Stand Up
RURAL
AMERICA

STAND UP RURAL AMERICA
Forging a New Path of Growth & Prosperity

Lorie Vincent, CEcD

Published by Game Changer Publishing

Paperback ISBN: 978-1-967424-69-6

Hardcover ISBN: 978-1-967424-70-2

Digital ISBN: 978-1-967424-71-9

GC | GAME CHANGER
PUBLISHING
www.GameChangerPublishing.com

This book is dedicated to all the Rural Changemakers and Trailblazers I've been fortunate to meet across the globe. You continue to inspire me every single day.

To my hometown of Dalhart, Texas, that gave me the best childhood a kid could ever hope for.

To the Sherman County Development Committee Board Members in Stratford, Texas, who took a chance on an idealistic young woman to help them grow. In doing so, they propelled me into a career that I grew to love, starting in a city that won my heart.

To my family and friends who have never wavered in their support of my crazy ideas and my relentless pursuit of action and celebration. They have encouraged me to believe that anyone can change the world for the better… one step at a time.

And to my fellow dreamer, Gerri Lawing, a beautiful heart that truly loved Rural America as much as I do. I miss you every day, dear friend. ♥

READ THIS FIRST

As a thank you for buying my book, I'd like to give you
a few bonuses/resources. My gift to you—no strings attached!

Scan the QR Code:

Stand Up RURAL AMERICA

LORIE VINCENT, CEcD

ACKNOWLEDGMENTS

"Lorie Vincent, with ACCELERATION by design, is a true champion for rural America. Her passion and dedication to uplifting rural communities shine through in everything she does. As a speaker and advocate, Lorie brings an unmatched energy and depth of experience, inspiring us with practical solutions and a heartfelt commitment to economic development. Her work through initiatives like the Stand Up Rural America Summit has empowered countless leaders, providing tangible tools to foster growth and collaboration. Lorie doesn't just talk about the potential of rural America—she actively accelerates it, making a lasting impact that resonates far beyond the stage."

–Charles Fitzgibbon
Conway Data, Inc.

"Rural communities face unique challenges. Lorie not only understood our challenges, but created workable, achievable solutions to help our town plan for directed growth and thrive! She continues to be an advocate for Rural America, and we couldn't be more thankful for her vision, support, and guidance."

–Katy Riddle
Greater Manchester Economic Development Board
Manchester, Tennessee

"Lorie Vincent fills an important niche in rural communities, whether through her consulting, her speaking engagements, or her Stand Up Rural America Summits. She provides information and expertise with boundless energy and enthusiasm. Lorie lives her passion empowering and encouraging economic developers, board members, elected officials, and community volunteers."

–Allison J. H. Thompson, CEcD EDFP
President/CEO
Economic Development Alliance for Jefferson County, Arkansas

ACKNOWLEDGMENTS

"Lorie Vincent, with ACCELERATION by design, is a true champion for rural America. Her passion and dedication to uplifting rural communities shine through in everything she does. As a speaker and advocate, Lorie brings an unmatched energy and depth of experience, inspiring us with practical solutions and a heartfelt commitment to economic development. Her work through initiatives like the Stand Up Rural America Summit has empowered countless leaders, providing tangible tools to foster growth and collaboration. Lorie doesn't just talk about the potential of rural America—she actively accelerates it, making a lasting impact that resonates far beyond the stage."

–Charles Fitzgibbon
Conway Data, Inc.

"Rural communities face unique challenges. Lorie not only understood our challenges, but created workable, achievable solutions to help our town plan for directed growth and thrive! She continues to be an advocate for Rural America, and we couldn't be more thankful for her vision, support, and guidance."

–Katy Riddle
Greater Manchester Economic Development Board
Manchester, Tennessee

"Lorie Vincent fills an important niche in rural communities, whether through her consulting, her speaking engagements, or her Stand Up Rural America Summits. She provides information and expertise with boundless energy and enthusiasm. Lorie lives her passion empowering and encouraging economic developers, board members, elected officials, and community volunteers."

–Allison J. H. Thompson, CEcD EDFP
President/CEO
Economic Development Alliance for Jefferson County, Arkansas

TABLE OF CONTENTS

LET'S DO *this*

OVER 30 YEARS AGO, I was introduced to the economic development industry. I had just eloped and moved to a small rural community in the Texas Panhandle. I did not know the town, my husband or what economic development even was. The community of Stratford, Texas, located in Sherman County, had just formed their first economic development committee. The committee, made up of community leaders, had been appointed by the county commissioners and tasked with forming an organization that would pursue economic vitality and prosperity for Sherman County residents.

Their first order of business? Hire an executive director. As luck would have it, I had just moved there and was working in a nearby city. I was approached by the committee to consider the position. I had a degree in Accounting and was trying to work out if I was going to stay married (that's another whole story!), what direction I was going to take my career, and what in the heck economic development even was.

The first thing I did was ask family and friends what they thought. The overwhelming consensus was, "You don't want to work for that board." What? I didn't know any of the people on the board, but after hearing that time and time again, I couldn't help but wonder what the foundation of this advice was. It was so prevalent. So, I made the rounds again and asked more probing questions. Why wouldn't I want to work for this board? Some thought it would be more financially viable to work for an accounting firm or in a position with a for-profit entity. But most shared with me that the board was loaded with the strongest and most assertive business leaders in the county. While they were all well-liked and well respected, they were hard task-maskers, had high expectations, had strong opinions, and were very action-oriented and anxious to get going. Instead of that scaring me off, it just intrigued me instead.

I told the EDC board that I didn't know anything about economic development. They said "Neither do we... we will learn together."

I'm so glad that I took the leap and made the decision to accept that first position as the Executive Director of the Sherman County Development Committee. From the very first day on the job, I was hooked. To wake up every day with the goal of making a positive difference in my community became a flame that burned hard and bright in me. And it was the launch of a career that expanded beyond my wildest dreams. In my 34-plus-year career in economic development, I've had the privilege of being a part of teams that have created tens of thousands of jobs and billions (with a B!) of dollars of capital investment. I've grown organizations at the local level, a large regional level, and at the state level. Together, we have built transformational industries, developed state-of-the-art industrial parks, created entrepreneurial programs, revitalized downtowns, expanded our existing businesses, and recruited prospects from across the globe.

The very first thing that my fresh, new Sherman County Development Board challenged me to do was to identify ten aspirational cities that we could learn from. Ten cities of a similar size, or a little larger, that were experiencing growth and vitality. I was to interview their leaders, compile their demographics, identify their economic drivers and report back to the board the initiatives that were transferable, or could be emulated. We were going to find what had worked elsewhere, and see if we could make it work for us, with an emphasis on rapid deployment and results.

The information that was gathered in the first year was invaluable to our organization. We took what we learned, developed a strong and ambitious program of work, and we were off and running. Sherman County Development has never looked back. After seven years, I moved into a position with our regional economic development organization. After 17 wonderful years with The High Ground of Texas, I was blessed with yet another chapter in my career. I moved into the lead position with Team Texas, tasked with taking a third organization to a new level of activity. It was an amazing three years of expansion for Team Texas. Finally, in 2018, following a long-time dream, I jumped into the deep end (with no floaties) and opened my own economic development consulting firm, ACCELERATION by design. It has been a head-spinning ride. Thirty-four years ago, I didn't even know such a career existed, or that I needed it. But it was made for me. Even through the hard times, I have loved every minute of it, along with the people I have had the honor and joy to work with.

As mentioned, over three decades ago, I began that study of aspirational cities. Every year since then, I have added approximately ten more cities to the study. This has given me a database of well over 300 rural communities across the U.S. that I have been studying for more than three decades. I have talked with them, interviewed their leaders, and compiled their data points. Most importantly, I have learned from them. I have been able to clearly recognize trends, identifying commonalities in those that were growing and determining why some were struggling. I was able to identify if fluctuations in their populations were due to organic growth or pursued growth. Was it due to changes in industries? Recessions? Natural Disasters? Aging populations? Tired schools? New residents? New industry? Local investment? Incentives? These observations from more than 300 cities, along with the 450+ cities I have directly worked with throughout my career, have provided a foundation of theories, trends, red flags, innovative ideas, and inspiration.

It's time for these observations to be shared. I can't promote it as a scientific study, because it was never set up in an officially accepted scientific format. (Remember, this started before the arrival of Google, Excel, Word, ChatGPT, and cell phones.) I started with landline rotary phones, handwritten notebooks, Rand McNally maps and Census Data that I found at the library. Instead, it's been a compilation of tangible research, filled with a collection of data points—population, school enrollment, number of businesses, infrastructure changes, water hook-ups, annexations, sales tax receipts, and more. I've had thousands of conversations in these cities with economic developers, chambers, mayors, board members, council members, county commissioners, volunteers, small businesses, and industry leaders.

At a minimum, this has led to the identification of various approaches that work, scenarios that don't, what makes a city special, and why some get stuck in the past and struggle to move forward. At most, it has provided an excellent way to take what works for others, make tweaks based on unique assets, and develop action plans built on sound, proven methods.

I have found myself sentimentally attached to and highly invested in the cities I have researched. No one makes it into my research pool without aligning with our original quest to study "aspirational and growing cities." However, I have watched many communities experience drastic changes. Some have stalled out and trended in the opposite direction. Some have continued to grow. Some have intentionally maintained their original population but pivoted to focus on specific aspects of their city to create a great quality of life. I've watched agricultural communities diversify and embrace new technologies. I've seen cities, sadly, struggle and decline due to natural or economic disasters. I have watched some cities with tremendous potential fail to get out of their own way. And I have watched cities grow so fast that they are stuck on a hamster wheel, constantly catching up with infrastructure.

Whew, boy, I've seen a lot.

This book is a candid compilation of my observations on several topics that affect rural economic development. Please note, I have had amazing experiences working on numerous projects in large metro areas and count an abundance of urban economic developers, site selectors, and industry leaders as both clients and friends. We have done great projects together, and will continue to do more.

But my heart is still with that little community that took a chance on me, with the 450+ rural communities I have had the privilege to work with, and with the 300+ rural communities I have been following for decades in my personal study. My heart will always be with the thousands of rural communities throughout the U.S. that may have all the ingredients they need to thrive but just don't have the tools, staff, or resources to pursue it.

Yet…

This book is for you. It's essentially the questions I would ask if you hired me to move your community toward growth and sustainability. It is written in a way that, if I were advising a board, a council, a committee, or just interested citizens, I'd simply say: TAKE ACTION. It's filled with questions, hard conversations, and calling out the elephants in the room. These challenging topics are necessary to move forward. But once addressed, they unlock opportunities for growth in ways you never imagined.

While my three decades of data research are being developed into a format I can publicly share, I wanted to start our conversation with the topics that are often barriers to growth—or beacons of opportunity. I promise you, if you ask yourself the questions I have put forth in this book—or better yet, if your local boards ask themselves these questions— you will be able to quickly and effectively take positive action. I have found that most communities want to jump straight to the part where visible growth happens while skipping the 20 steps necessary to get there first. This book will help guide your thought process.

We have to work extra hard to pursue economic development in Rural America. We have to be extra vigilant, extra resourceful, extra loud, and highly creative. The most important thing I have learned is: DON'T wait until your ducks are in a row, your funding is perfect, or your community is ready.

Just start. Take action. Do something positive. Start moving the train forward. Do a few things, and then you'll watch it pick up speed. People will jump on the train and enthusiasm will create a path to growth that you never saw coming.

This book is for those who are tired of talking and ready to start doing. Stand Up, Rural America! Let's go!

TAKING STOCK...

RURAL IS A
state of mind

I CAN TELL YOU RIGHT NOW: there is no nationally accepted population threshold that determines whether a city is rural or not. It's easy to identify a city of 500 or 5,000 as rural. But what if a city of 15,000 is on a major interstate? They will have opportunities that other rural communities won't. What if a city has only 10,000 people, but a metro city that used to be 30 miles away has now grown to just 10 miles away? What if a city has a population of 50,000 but is over 75 miles from the nearest metro area or airport?

Over the years, I've worked with programs such as the EDA, USDA, SBA, CDBG funds, the Texas Capital Fund, and more, and I can attest that there is no universally accepted population number or formula that defines whether a community is "rural." Each program uses a different formula.

More importantly, if a community considers itself rural, it is. If they don't, then they probably aren't going to pursue programs designed for rural communities. I have often joked that if you can't catch an Uber from the airport to your hotel, you're probably rural. The point is that numbers don't matter—unless you're applying for a funding program or grant.

Rural communities generally have a few things in common, both positive and challenging. They are filled to the brim with people who are innovative, resourceful, and extremely proud of their heritage. They do not take kindly to being told they can't do something, they are quick to volunteer, and they are very nimble when it comes to using available resources.

However, economic or community development programs in rural areas are sometimes very small or even nonexistent. Funding is limited, and tools are not always readily available. Often, the person tasked with economic development wears many hats—economic development, local events, business development, downtown revitalization, and more. In small communities, there are often those who remember "how it used to be" instead of opening their minds to "what it can be now."

Having a Rural State of Mind is a wonderful blend of history, heritage, and pride—understanding why the community exists, who makes up its population, and what makes it so special. It's not just about numbers; it's about geographic location, distance or proximity to metro areas, and infrastructure, such as medical services and transportation hubs. It's about culture and building on an existing business base. It's about understanding the challenges of growing a small community while embracing the very factors that make each one unique.

We can't get hung up on the number that defines "rural." Let's embrace our destiny and move forward with growth and sustainability strategies that will help each community shine to its fullest potential.

WHAT RURAL
means to me

THROUGHOUT MY CAREER, I have worked in the smallest of cities (population 250) to the largest of states (Texas!) and everything in between. There is one thing we all have in common, regardless of population: our quest to live and work in a place that is safe, beautiful, and filled with the amenities that feed our desired quality of life.

There are many reasons why people choose to live where they live or work where they work. It might be arts and culture, or it might be recreational opportunities. It might be proximity to medical care or the opportunity to live and work near family. It might be because of the reputation of an excellent school district or the affordability of housing. But something we all have in common is the desire for a beautiful environment, safe streets, and friendly neighbors. We want proximity to shopping for everyday needs and quality gathering spaces to be with friends and neighbors.

I grew up in a rural community (Dalhart, Texas). It was like Mayberry to me. We lived at the end of a street where the neighborhood kids gathered. It bumped up against a beautiful canyon that we explored throughout our childhood. We had a vibrant downtown, a beautiful lake, a great school system, and a solid business base.

To a child, it was perfect. I wouldn't trade my childhood for anything. It was only later in life that I learned of the challenges that the community faced to remain dynamic and healthy. The economic basis of the community was agriculture, so there were years of drought and years of bountiful harvests. It was big enough that the community leadership did not always have the same vision for growth and sustainability. The lake was man-made and fed by water wells that were expensive and hard to maintain.

While benefactors were generous in the building of a hospital and medical facilities, it was a challenge to attract (and keep) doctors and medical professionals in the small, remote community. While the downtown of my childhood was dynamic and bustling with activity, the stores began to experience the challenges of mail-order goods, the limited population base, competition for goods from nearby cities, and a younger generation moving away for jobs and opportunities.

On the one hand, the city was filled with heritage, pride, and people who would work hard to keep the city moving forward. They worked to get improved highways, newer schools and stadiums, more housing, and quality medical facilities. They diversified the agriculture industry base and began to build businesses that would attract people off multiple highways that diverged in the city. I am so proud of the city I grew up in, but equally proud of the city it is today. They have fought to maintain their identity and celebrate their heritage, and it remains a great place to live, work, and retire.

After moving to another small city for college (Kerrville, Texas) and then to a metro area to work (San Antonio, Texas), I began to see the stark differences. Not better and not worse, but different. Suddenly, I had access to a convenience store on every block. I learned about the benefits of public transportation, easily accessible medical care, an abundance of choices for restaurants, entertainment, and housing.

But it also wasn't as easy to meet your neighbors. I had to be more careful about where I went, where I parked, and who I talked to. I had a tremendous amount of good luck and bad luck during those years as I figured out how to find my way in the world. I loved the energy and amenities of the city, but I missed the connection to my hometown. My awesome friends from my youth are still my friends today. Some stayed, and some left, but we are bound by our shared experiences of fun, adventure, school activities, and a life blissfully unaware of cell phones, the internet, Google, texting, or GPS. It was magical.

Through a crazy and unpredictable series of events, I found myself married (after an impulsive elopement) and living in a rural community again (Stratford, Texas). As I pondered my life choices and began to plan my escape route, the craziest thing happened. I found myself drawn back into the lifestyle that I had loved so much as a child and teenager. The gift of caring neighbors, friendships for every stage of life, and a school system that would develop our children into amazing young contributors to society. A community filled with churches, events, and sports. A community filled with people who loved where they lived and had no intention of ever leaving.

That rural community embraced me, and I began to love it back. But as I got involved in the economic development side of the business, I began—now as an adult—to see more clearly the challenges our rural communities face. Retiring businesses, aging infrastructure, and increased mobility were creating competition for goods in nearby towns. An economic base dependent on commodity prices, rainfall, and favorable weather added to the strain. There was no lack of pride in the community, but there were certainly challenges in maintaining it, growing it, and celebrating it.

After more than three decades in the economic development industry at every population level, my heart lies most with the rural communities that are filled with people who want to stay, want to help, want to grow, want to raise their families there, want to have a business there, and want to retire there. I'm with you, I feel you and I understand you.

But to do this, we have to be realistic about what growth and sustainability means to our communities.

It's not about taking our cities back to the heyday of our youth. It's about creating a community that will thrive with today's challenges and opportunities.

We cannot "recreate" the city you grew up in, but we can take what's beautiful and special about it, where you are, and what assets you have, and create a thriving city of today and tomorrow.

After she graduated from college, my daughter took a job several states away in Rhinelander, Wisconsin—and she wasn't afraid. She went to the initial interview alone and fell in love with the city, the people, and the beautiful surroundings. I was surprised—and a little dismayed—that she was moving so far from us. But she said the community was special. And I felt it, too.

Then she moved to another city nearby (Merrill, Wisconsin) as she furthered her career and prepared to marry a Wisconsin fella. I asked her if she would be satisfied living in another rural community. After all, I loved my adventures in the city. But she said it felt like home. And I agreed with her. It's another beautiful small town in central Wisconsin that shared so many of the awesome traits that we all love about Rural America. A wonderful place to live, raise a family, and build a thriving business.

I had the privilege of growing up in an amazing rural community, marrying into another amazing rural community, working with hundreds of rural communities in Texas, and then working with hundreds of communities with my consulting firm. There are many similarities between them, including the challenges, but they are all unique in what makes each one special.

I'm not saying that our good friends who live in the metro areas don't feel the same pride in their cities because they do, and they should. And I share their enthusiasm for loving where they live.

But there is something special about Rural America.

Let's embrace it. Grow it. And celebrate it.

LOCAL *leadership*

I AM VERY MUCH AN ACTION-ORIENTED PERSON, so I usually don't get into the weeds on the topic of local leadership. I believe anyone can take action in a community, and most improvements do not need the approval or permission of a board or council to move forward. I've seen many communities grow and make huge improvements in their community with, without, or in spite of local leadership.

That's not to say that the support of local leadership is not critical in most large projects. That is not the case. But the biggest slow-down or drag on progress is when a community waits for permission to take action.

Often, the areas that need the most improvements impact private property. Therefore, unless there is a specific policy that would assist or affect the action, there's no need for the involvement of the city or county.

However, when it comes to infrastructure needs, planning and zoning adjustments, the enforcement of ordinances, the impact on easements and public property, taxing entities, and more, it is essential to work with local taxing jurisdictions and leadership to create initiatives that address specific needs.

It is also critical to have the support of local leadership for any formal or informal initiatives planned or underway by the economic development board, chamber of commerce, downtown revitalization group, or clean-up committee. This isn't necessarily about seeking permission but rather securing public support. Consistent and positive communication—keeping local leadership informed of planned projects, initiatives, and funding needs—ensures that everyone remains involved in some capacity. It also allows local leaders to answer community questions accurately and provide status updates. Most importantly, many federal and utility grants require a city or county sponsor. It's far better to involve stakeholders from the beginning than to seek their support late in the process.

A simple piece of advice: Prepare a monthly or quarterly status report for all local leadership groups to review at their regular board meetings. It doesn't need to be lengthy or overly detailed—just a short paragraph describing the current status of projects. Include the intended outcome, timeline, partners involved, and the expected impact on the community. This prevents surprises, keeps leadership in the loop, and fosters continued support as they track the project's progress. Most importantly, it ensures that everyone receives the same information at the same time, reducing rumors, speculation, and discrepancies about project status. Clear, consistent talking points are highly effective in keeping everything on track.

Lesson Learned: Be aware of what is confidential information and involves prospect or company negotiations and financial information. This information is not to be shared in public forums and can instantly kill a project. But keeping your local leadership "in the know" on the status of most projects will result in trust, confidence and the expansion of support between the affected organizations. It will also give you the ability to answer questions or head off any negativity towards the projects ahead of time and in the appropriate forum.

CITIZEN
engagement

LET'S FACE IT: good things can happen to most communities, sometimes planned, sometimes by happenstance. For example, you might have an unusually large event, resulting in more people learning about your shops, restaurants, and quality of life. Or you might have an alumni of the community give a surprise donation to the local library, school, parks, or business efforts. A new banker may be supportive of new programs for small businesses. New residents may volunteer to create new programs for the youth. Any number of things can happen that will provide some juice and enthusiasm to the community. The more difficult challenge is: how do you sustain that feeling of enthusiasm and pride? How do you encourage others to join in the efforts?

While the local elected leadership may have control over the resources, it is the citizenry itself that are the key to the creation and sustainability of good initiatives.

They hold the key to momentum.

The spark that keeps it going.

The elected leaders can fund it, support it, and change or create policy for it. But it is the citizens themselves who will sustain it.

So how do we get the citizens engaged? We've found a couple of things that work:

1. We do what we say we are going to do. No more concepts, no more theories, no more wondering, no more guessing, no more talking. Just do something. You don't need a big elaborate plan to get action going. It can be as simple as painting dumpsters with the high school art class. Planting flowers on Main Street. Picking up trash after events. Sweeping sidewalks and washing windows. Appreciating your local businesses. It can be a small effort or a big initiative. Just do *something* positive that moves the train forward.

2. We include our citizens in our discussions and our decision-making. I have worked in cities that hold their meetings on weekdays during work hours to discourage citizen engagement in their city council or economic development board meetings. I have worked in cities that meet in small board or conference rooms to make it uncomfortable for interested citizens to participate in the meetings. When this is intentional, it is disheartening. We do not need to discourage citizen participation; we should be encouraging it. Ask the citizens to share what they know about specific topics. Encourage discussion between the boards and councils and the citizens they serve. If everyone is respectful of each other, amazing things can happen in a community. No, you won't agree on everything, but at least decisions can be made in an informed manner with full input of all sides' perspectives. I can assure you that if you discourage citizen engagement where decisions about the future of the community are being made, the discussion is taking place at the coffee shop without you, and this does nothing but slow down progress and growth. Promote an open and honest process, and you will be amazed at how quickly citizen engagement can turn into enthusiastic action.

3. We ask the citizens what is important to them. We ask them how they are doing. What are their needs? What are they buying when they leave town on the weekends? Ask the students what they would like to see in their community. Ask the senior citizens what services or programs can make their lives better. Ask the young families about childcare, school programs, and recreation opportunities. Ask the business and industry stakeholders what the city, county, EDC, and Chamber of Commerce can do to

help them be successful. Most importantly, ask them why they love where they live. And if they don't, why not?

4. Include all segments of the community in the discussions. Some of my favorite meetings are with high school students who are very honest about what it would take for them to stay or come back to their community after graduation. What are they looking for? What do they feel like they are missing that other cities might have? Most of all, what do they love about their community? What would they miss if they left? Their answers will amaze you. They are thoughtful, frank, sometimes naïve, but honest. The conversations are always helpful. Ask the senior citizens what needs they have in this season of life. Are they being met? Could we be doing more? What would cause them to leave? What amenities would allow them to stay? Ask the minority groups in the community if their livability needs are being met. What are some barriers that can be addressed? What do they love about living in their community?

5. And my best advice on this topic: We often only listen to the people who are most engaged—sitting on boards, elected officials, businesses owners, etc. Get everyone's engagement. Meet them where they're at. Go to the school. Go to the senior center. Go to the churches. Go to the fundraisers. Go to the block parties. Go to the daycare center. Go to the park. Go to where the citizens are, and you will find a goldmine of feedback. You might not love all of it, but it will be important information that will help you tailor your economic development initiatives moving forward. I promise you, you are going to be surprised by some of the answers. More importantly, you are going to hear, time and time again, the statements, "No one has ever asked me" or "Thank you for asking me." Just because someone doesn't go to every city council meeting, EDC meeting, or chamber meeting doesn't mean they don't care about the future of their community. They just need to be invited to the conversation and feel like they have been heard. It is an effort worth pursuing.

In my research, I consistently found that the most vibrant cities were those with high citizen engagement. This was not an accident—it was entirely intentional. Things aren't always unicorns, sprinkles, and cupcakes, but dealing with serious concerns, along with positive issues, keeps the door open for progress and for quick resolutions to issues. This creates an environment for community growth and palpable enthusiasm for where people live.

Every taxpayer is an investor in the community. Give them a voice and a seat at the table. The risk is worth the reward.

Example: In one of my client communities, we initiated a "student town hall meeting" to discuss their vision for their community. Their engagement was invigorating and imaginative. And more importantly, it was mostly plausible. But to take it a step further, the students decided to create their own project, asking the citizens of the community what they loved about their city. People are always quick to point out what they don't love, but we rarely ask them what they do love.

Each student asked ten people in their lives what they loved about their community, and they captured the interviews on video. They also asked interviewees what they didn't like about the community. They just asked interviewees to name three things they felt the community could work on, but this was not recorded. When you're asking them the tough questions, people are a lot more candid when they're not on camera!

The students then pulled all of their video clips together, edited them into one presentation and then showed it all over the community. Different students presented it to the city council, the county commissioners, the EDC, the chamber, the business groups, the school board, the senior citizens, the churches, the nursing home, the coffee shops...anywhere that they could get an audience. They interviewed their parents, their neighbors, their grandparents, their friends, local businesses, their teachers, their mailman, their banker, strangers on the street.

It was amazing. Not only did it instill a huge sense of pride in their community, but they all felt closer for having shared what they loved—which was the same answer that so many others gave. And through their candid conversations about what they would change, some issues were brought to light that the elected officials had not even been aware of.

I did not put them up to this project. It was totally organic. I had the best seat in the house to watch it unfold. It's been several years now since they initiated the project, and when I check back in on them, it's obvious that it was an important factor in getting the community off the fence and the catalyst for some very productive projects.

In all honesty, this project worked precisely because it *was not* a community survey that was done on social media, sent by email, or promoted on TikTok. It was a human conversation between people who care. From various generations and perspectives. Such a novel approach!

You have amazing people in every block of your community. Invite them all to the party!

CREATING *True livability*

LIVABILITY FACTORS DEFINE THE REASONS why someone chooses to live in a specific city or region—or chooses not to. The most common livability factors include clean air and water, safe neighborhoods, social interaction and gathering places, vibrant business districts, utilities and services, parks and recreation, affordability and cost of living, connectivity, arts and culture, and diversity. In other words, there's little point in working on other initiatives if your strongest livability factors are in peril, declining, or nonexistent. A city, chamber, county, school, hospital district, and economic development corporation (EDC) can all work on various quality-of-life initiatives simultaneously, but these core livability factors are the primary drivers that measure a city's health and sustainability.

Livability blooms from the bottom up, not the top down. It cannot simply be planned—it must be cultivated organically. It requires local vision, commitment, forward-thinking initiatives, and a strong sense of civic responsibility.

Many believe that people's love for where they live fuels their desire to improve and enhance it. The impact of the environment on public health, civic pride, and economic well-being is critical. Heritage is also a unique asset—every community, large or small, has a distinctive character shaped by its history. A community's demographic and social makeup, natural and man-made environments, and the combination of public and private institutions can either create or inhibit opportunities for expanding and nurturing quality of life.

A community that meets the full range of its residents' needs is more attractive as a place to live, work, and do business — making it more likely to be economically successful and sustainable.

Taking an opportunity-focused approach instead of a problem-focused one is essential for community viability and sustainability. Building an economic development vision that celebrates and builds on existing assets will take you further and faster than dwelling on what the community lacks. An optimistic, entrepreneurial approach to problem-solving — rather than endless problem analysis or complaints — is essential for fostering goodwill and collaboration.

Action speaks louder than planning.

Lesson Learned: Declare success frequently. Nothing has a better chance for success than a situation in which people can participate, contribute, and claim ownership of good civic ideas. Stop and celebrate. As in any marathon, there must be places of rest; places where there is cause for a party to acknowledge achievement and to renew determination to succeed. A small victory, every quarter or six months, should be built into a program to create the pleasure of success and the commitment to keep going.

High fives and shout-outs all around!

LONG-TIMERS VS.
The new citizen

OUR CITIES ROCK ALONG FINE with the families and residents that have seen it through decades of growth, decline, celebration, heartache, growth, droughts, resurgence, good football teams, and disappointing seasons. They have lived through vibrant downtowns and empty buildings. Through new schools and old schools. Through heartache and jubilation. There is something special about those who have lived somewhere their whole lives, came back to raise their family, or moved there because of family heritage or history.

But then, a company expands, and new people arrive. The school grows, so new teachers move in. Businesses close because the long-time owner passes away with no heirs to take it over. And then someone from a nearby city buys the business and re-opens it. While it doesn't always feel like it, our cities are in a constant state of flux. It can be growing, or it can be shrinking, but we all know that the status quo does not exist. It's how we handle it moving forward that dictates the health of our cities.

We must remove the distrust between long-time residents and new residents. I often see the current residents dig in their heels and treat the newcomers with skepticism, already thinking that they want to "change" things. I often see new residents come in hot with all the ways they think things can be "improved." Oh goodness, this is so predictable. Getting the two groups to collaborate is often a very tricky thing.

The first thing we must do is welcome the new people to our cities.

News flash to long-time citizens: Your community will not survive without new residents. Regardless of the size of your city—rural, suburbs, or urban—you are going to lose population through attrition. People pass away or move away. Fewer babies are being born in our country. We are not able to sustain our local populations only with the citizens that are "from there."

But even more importantly, while long-time residents get all the credit for keeping their cities alive to this point, it's a new world out there. They often see their cities "how they used to be" and perhaps also don't see the condition of their city "now" clearly. It takes fresh eyes to see the assets and opportunities that exist with no history to slant, minimize, or sentimentalize their impressions.

News flash to new residents: You didn't build this community from scratch. You didn't toil over building infrastructure, schools, streets, lights, churches, and parks. It wasn't your hard-earned taxes that created this community. So please give grace to those who have an intense and deep love of their community. It is often hard to fathom the passion that people have for a city that has raised generations of the same family.

Let's face it: to have a healthy, vibrant, and inclusive community, it takes current *and* new residents. The long-time members bring history, heritage, pride, wisdom, and perspective. The new members bring new dollars, fresh ideas, examples of what has worked in other cities, and enthusiasm for future growth.

It takes all of these things, mixed together like a stew, to create initiatives to not only maintain population, but become a sustainable and healthy community.

I've never been a proponent of telling a community that they must grow. Many citizens truly love the size of their cities, the size of their schools, and their quality of life. But you also need to be realistic about the numbers. You are always going to lose some population through events beyond your control. You've got to be open to the idea of new people moving in to maintain that population you love so much. And then you need to be realistic about the types of services and businesses that your population can support.

We now live in a world in which everything can be shipped overnight. Even to your rural address. People have different eating patterns. Different transportation needs. Different housing needs.

So basically, what I'm saying is: You cannot stand still.

You can build and maintain the community that you love and the quality of life that you love, but it takes thriving businesses, affordable housing, active leadership, and strong citizen engagement.

Old investment and new investment. Old perspective and fresh ideas. Long-standing traditions and new cultures.

We can grow Rural America.

But only if we do it together.

IT'S OKAY TO *diversify*

THE RURAL AMERICA OF TODAY is not the Rural America of yesteryear. It is very easy for each of us to expound on what we love about our communities. We can extoll the fabulous memories of our youth. After all, if you are reading this book, you are probably from Rural America or living in Rural America.

We share the same passion for a thriving Rural America.

But it's a big country. Our competition for businesses, jobs, capital investment, and residents are not with the hundreds of metro areas in the U.S., but with the tens of thousands of rural communities that make up most of the country.

I have had the privilege of working in over 450 rural communities throughout the country, and have been researching over 300 rural communities for over three decades.

It is very important, especially in this day and age, to realize one thing. It's okay to diversify.

It's necessary to diversify to expand your industrial and business base. Perhaps a long-time agriculture community is now expanding to attract remote workers or advanced technology. Perhaps a community that has long been a bedroom community to a metro area now has the opportunity to attract tourism and a younger population. Perhaps a community that is blessed with natural resources now invests in outdoor recreation initiatives in order to maintain and grow its population. Perhaps a small community that enjoyed numerous retail businesses 30 years ago can transform into a tech hub or a training center for the region.

Nothing stays the same.

You can be an agriculture-based community and still welcome advanced manufacturing.

You can be a manufacturing community and still attract tourism.

You can be a tourism-based community and still develop a supply chain industrial park.

You can have thriving industrial parks and still attract boutique downtown businesses.

You can have a vibrant downtown and still recruit commercial businesses on your highways.

It's not an either/or proposition. It's about expanding your economic base in a smart and intentional way. Our populations are not one-dimensional, and your business base needn't be either. Embrace that you have the opportunity to expand your community's economic base beyond "what it's always been."

In this case, it's a good thing *not* to have all your eggs in one basket. A diversified economy will provide an expanded variety of jobs and help your community weather the ups and downs in the uncertainty of financial markets, weather, commodity prices, and consumer demand.

WHO'S IN *charge?*

THOSE OF US WHO WORK in rural communities often wear multiple hats. Even though this is the case, it is very important that we are clear on who is wearing what hat at any given time.

Economic Development and Community Development do not "just happen." There's a process. Granted, some things may happen organically, and that's great, but you can't depend on good things just materializing by luck or osmosis.

Because the resources and available labor are often sparse, different people may be approached about specific opportunities or programs.

Consider the following:
- Who is the person in your community who can have that economic development project conversation, act upon it, and see it through?
- Do you have a paid economic developer?
- If not, does the Chamber of Commerce handle this—or the city manager? Or the mayor?
- Do you have a volunteer committee or a volunteer board?
- Do you even know if anyone has the role of economic or community development in their job description?

Who oversees economic development? If you, as a stakeholder in the community, don't know, how will prospective employers, prospects, residents, etc. know?

Most importantly, the team members who work at the convenience stores, hotels, and restaurants need to know who that person is. They are often the first conversation someone has when personally visiting your city.

I will always contend that I have been successful in my career because I have had the privilege of being paid to get up every day and work towards the mission. Every day. It was my job to pursue the mission and objectives of the organization and my community, region, or state every single day. There was never any doubt or question about who to contact. That singular focus can certainly pay dividends. But it's not always feasible or realistic in small rural communities. However, if you can direct this function to a specific person, you will see considerably more tangible progress than if you don't.

That said, regardless of who is responsible for pursuing economic or community development initiatives in the community, make sure that "someone" is trained to take the call. If it's a volunteer, give them the tools and permission to act. If it's a board or committee, make sure there are processes in place for who will handle what. If it's a paid economic developer, make sure they have accountability and reporting policies in place.

The turnaround time for projects, decisions, and actions is drastically shorter than it was just ten years ago. There is no time to run the table in a rural community "looking" for someone who can provide economic development assistance. If someone needs to call more than two people looking for the right person to talk to, then I can assure you that you are losing opportunities left and right.

I have just discussed what happens if someone reaches out to you. But the more critical question is: Who is doing outreach on behalf of the community to get people interested in the opportunities your community has to offer? If someone in the community isn't doing outreach, then anything good that happens is an accident. You can get lucky now and then, but you can't rely on luck for sustainability and growth.

For an organization to be effective in both internal and external initiatives, it is important to develop and maintain a set of community, county, and regional information that is used in decision-making, prospecting, prospect responses, small business development, marketing outreach, measurability of initiatives, and more. These records should be updated on a regular basis and be stored in a manner that allows them to be accessed quickly, digitally, and in a professional reporting format. Someone needs to maintain and mind the store.

Bonus: Please click on the QR code at the front or back of the book for a List of the Records that should be maintained for economic development activities.

Questions to Consider:

- If someone calls your city hall or chamber of commerce to discuss an economic development opportunity, who does the call get directed to?
- Who is doing outside marketing to potential employers, residents, or investors?
- Who is doing internal marketing to the citizens of the community?
- Who is arranging and hosting prospect visits?
- Who is securing the conversations with people a potential business or resident would like to talk to?
- Who is building relationships with your current business base?
- What if a local citizen is interested in opening a business in the community?
- Do you have a website or marketing materials that clearly state who the contact is?

Know who is responsible for economic development strategies. If no one is currently responsible for growth initiatives, you are leaving the future of your community to chance.

WHO IS SPEAKING
for the community?

WHEN EXPLORING NEW GROWTH INITIATIVES, attracting new businesses, or welcoming new residents, it's vital that the message is clear and consistent.

I will never forget an event that happened in the mid-1990s in my rural community. I was driving back from a doctor's appointment in Amarillo, about 85 miles away. I heard on the radio that the highways were closed outside of Stratford due to an ammonia spill on the rail line. It was hazardous, and they evacuated the whole north side of the town until it was resolved. I stopped at the house of a friend who lived about five miles south of town.

While we were there, we saw on their television that many of the regional media stations were interviewing people who were hanging out at the county barn on the south side of town. I recognized all of the people in the background, but none of the people who were being interviewed. I saw the mayor, three of my EDC board members, the president of the local bank, the owner of the local grain company, and the school superintendent. They were all standing in the background, visiting with each other, while the interviews were taking place.

Instead of stepping up and offering to talk to the cameras, we saw interviews with people who were *not* in the know. People who were not positive ambassadors of the community. People who were mad about being displaced. People who rarely leave their homes. People who gave erroneous information about the situation. Travelers who called the town

"Hicksville" and the "Armpit of the World." One person even said they couldn't wait to get out of Oklahoma—they didn't even know what state they were in!

As the local economic developer, I could not have been more mortified. This was "before" everyone had cell phones, so I couldn't even call anyone to rectify the situation. This was before TikTok, Facebook, YouTube, and Instagram (thank goodness!). Instead, I had to stand there and watch every bad image and erroneous stereotype of Rural America paraded across the screen, listening to the community being badmouthed by people who never talk about it otherwise. It was on the regional 6:00 pm, 10:00 pm, breaking news, morning news, and next day noon segments. In living color. For all of prosperity.

It was my worst nightmare. Seriously, almost 30 years later, I still vividly remember everything about that evening. I remember their words and their impressions. I resolved right then and there that the media would *always* know who to talk to from that point forward. I resolved that every local stakeholder would have talking points that would allow them to speak comfortably and confidently to any media, prospect, investor, or guest who had questions about our community. I had video that I obtained from the television stations to show the EDC board, the city council, the chamber, the school board, and the county commissioners, showing *why* it is important to step in and be a positive ambassador of the community. It was a hard lesson learned. A very hard lesson learned.

Our small community was filled with nationally renowned businessmen and women, educated professionals, extremely innovative and forward-thinking farmers and ranchers, vibrant small businesses, accomplished leaders, spirited volunteers, and people who passionately love their city. Where were they when the cameras broke out? Where were they in a time of crisis? Where were they when their words and articulation were so desperately needed?

Standing in the background.

Rural America is special. And we know it. But are we using our megaphone to tell everyone how great we are?

The most dynamic rural communities across our country have a chorus of residents who are positive spokespeople for their cities, schools, hospitals, leaders and neighbors. They may all sing a different tune, but it is positive and impactful.

We can't stop the occasional disgruntled citizen from speaking out. And for some reason, when they do, there will be a camera nearby—I can promise you that. And honestly, occasionally, they have valid points to make. But it is important for the world to hear the "rest of the story."

The good story.

If you aren't singing the praises of your community, then you are leaving yourself open to someone else sharing your story for you. It may be a competitor. It may be nefarious. It may just be that this is all they know. But in the absence of your positive talking points, you are invisible and vulnerable.

Are you speaking up? Speaking out? Speaking Loud?

You have a great story. Craft it. Share it. And repeat it.

Again. And again. And again.

BUILDING YOUR
basic needs

IT'S TIME TO TAKE STOCK. To have a truly sustainable community, it's important to look under the hood. To check on the engine. To gauge how well it's running. Just like it's important to keep a car's engine running smoothly with regular oil changes and tune-ups, it's important to take note of your community's engine.

There are basic needs in every community that must be met to keep it on the path of vitality. Basic needs are tangible. We will talk about attitude, apathy, and enthusiasm later. For the sake of this point, I'm talking about the true basic needs that form the foundation of your quality of life.

There are four of these basic needs:
- Adequate Housing
- Quality Education
- Access to Medical Care
- Reliable Connectivity

Of course, there are other needs that every community must address, but these are the underlying factors that provide the foundation. Remember, these basic needs and other needs can be addressed simultaneously or grouped into strong initiatives.

Often, directing attention to the basic needs is either "not my job," or we think that others are "taking care of those things." And yes, while these four topics may not fall under the purview of the city or economic development board, it is important that we know where we stand, the availability of these needs, and how to articulate the status of them to our local and prospective residents and businesses. It is when we assume that someone else will tend to it that we find ourselves with substandard housing, limited medical care, declining schools, and inadequate connectivity.

By ensuring that these four factors are the basis of planning, collaboration, and outreach, you will build a foundation on which other contributing factors can flourish: parks and recreation, cultural activities, revitalized downtowns, special events, small business development, industry recruitment, and more.

#1: Adequate Housing

Safe and affordable housing is a must. A vibrant community obviously offers a variety of housing options. However, at the very least, you must start with an inventory of safe and affordable housing.

- Do you know the status of your inventory?
- What type of housing do you have?
- What is the percentage of available vs. unavailable?
- What is the condition, age, and value of the inventory?
- Are there any prevalent problems that exist prohibiting new housing development?
- Utility issues?
- Funding issues?
- Attractive site issues?
- Do you offer both single-family housing and multi-family housing?
- Mobile home parks?
- Second-story living?
- Senior housing?
- Assisted living?
- Tiny homes?
- Who can be contacted if someone is in need of housing?
- Is there a local clearinghouse, online board, or realtor group?

Your community cannot grow without adequate housing to meet the needs of your current population, with its demographics and average income.

It's much easier to attract investors for additional housing when your community is thriving than waiting until the need is critical and urgent.

But not all housing is created equal. Therefore, when a community gives the rallying cry of "We need housing," there's an abundance of questions that need to be answered. Technically, there are more than twenty types of housing to consider, including the following:

- Single-family starter homes to rent
- Single-family starter homes to buy
- Single-family custom homes to buy
- Multi-family residential to buy
- Multi-family residential to rent
- Duplex/Fourplexes to buy
- Duplex/Fourplexes to rent
- Townhomes/Condos to buy
- Townhomes/Condos to rent
- Senior active 55+ residential to rent
- Senior active 55+ Garden homes to buy
- Independent living complexes
- Assisted living complexes
- Long-term care facilities
- Modular homes
- Mobile home parks
- Tiny homes to rent
- Tiny homes to buy
- Mixed-use rentals/Lofts
- Second-story living
- Portable worker housing
- Long-term RV parks
- Vacation rentals
- And more...

These various housing initiatives all require a different level of investment, have different incentive programs available to developers, and constitute a very diverse level of affordability.

One of the biggest mistakes I see in communities across the U.S. is investing in housing the community wants, instead of the type of housing the community needs. I'm highly supportive of proactively investing in the types of neighborhoods that match the vision of a community, but only if the overall economic development plan aggressively supports the efforts to create jobs at a salary that can support that type of housing. Otherwise, you will be left with empty homes and angry developers, and you will not have solved your problem of providing housing that meets your immediate needs.

A strong housing market helps families build wealth, attend good schools, and live in communities that are more conducive to long-term success. When you are ready to discuss the "need for housing" in your community, be sure to drill down to identify your actual needs.

Also remember that housing availability is a chain reaction. In developing your housing flow chart, consider that inserting new housing opportunities at any level of the inventory will start a domino effect opening up housing at a different level. A well-planned and maintained housing forecast is critical to the viability and sustainability of a community.

Lesson Learned: Give serious thought to your actual market when identifying your housing needs, and be willing to invest dollars into the resurgence of historical and long-standing neighborhoods to increase the overall quality of life in your community. It is possible to build new neighborhoods and revitalize vintage neighborhoods at the same time. Just as we all like our eggs cooked a different way, so goes our preference for housing. Please don't assume that everyone wants to live in the same type of housing—or can afford the same type of housing. A healthy, vibrant community will have a whole buffet of housing options to meet the needs of its citizens.

#2: Quality Education

I've never worked or lived in a community where the school system wasn't a priority.

It may seem clichéd to say "Our children are our future," but it's true. Our children *are* our future: our future labor force, future entrepreneurs, future public servants, and future leaders. It is our obligation, as a community, to provide them with the best tools and learning environments to reach their maximum potential.

In economic development, we look at the educational environment in three ways: (1) as a measure of a healthy community; (2) as a quality-of-life issue; and (3) as a recruiting tool for growth.

As a professional economic developer, I would pose the following questions to the citizens of your community:

- Is your school system an asset to the community?
- Is it a viable and healthy environment for learning?
- Is it a safe and engaging atmosphere for the students, teachers, and administration?
- What is the physical condition of your facilities, food service, parking, HVAC and technology?
- Is your community able to recruit and retain a superior level of teaching professionals?
- Is your school environment competitive with other school systems and other employers in the region?
- Do the schools in your community provide the highest level of technology needed in today's digital world?
- Is your school system a reason people live in your community, or is it the reason people leave your community?
- Do school activities bring the community together?
- Do extracurricular activities bring outside tourism into your community?
- Can your school system absorb a growth in population and additional students, or is it at capacity?
- Do you know how many additional students can be absorbed into the system before major improvements, facility expansions, or new staff are needed?
- Is there a vision for administration to make it the best it can be?

- Does the school system have bond capacity to make improvements?

A strong educational system is a critical pillar for economic growth and prosperity. The underlying objective of economic development is to create jobs, secure capital investment, increase the tax base, and grow the population to support your existing and new business base. If economic development efforts are to be successful, the excellence of the school system will have played its part.

However, if your community is in decline or you have experienced a loss of population, the condition of the local school systems will be significantly affected by the subsequent loss of tax base. It's not that the community doesn't want more for their schools, it's that they don't have the budget for it. For people to stay in a community, or for new residents to want to live in your community, a thriving school system is critical to the city's foundation. Modern technology, qualified teachers, and safe and adequate structures are required.

No, it's not the job of the economic developer to monitor and improve the school system. But it is important for the economic development board and the city leaders to be involved in the conversation, the forward planning, and the efforts to maintain an excellent school system.

Can you use their enrollment numbers, graduation rates, test scores, innovative programs, etc. in marketing? If not, you have an issue. Can you help in recruiting teachers and administration? Can you support programs that partner the schools with local industry to promote career paths? Can you comfortably include information about the school programs in your presentations? If not, then this factor, this basic need, has room for improvement.

Likewise, your schools may be operating at a level of excellence but may have trouble recruiting the teachers and support staff that it needs to maintain it. The issue may be the quality of life of the community, the job availability for trailing spouses, or the opportunity to find quality and affordable housing. These issues do fall under the umbrella of economic development efforts. Everyone has a role in the viability of the education system in the community. Be a team player and help where you can!

I have often said that if a downtown is the *heart* of your community, then the school system is your *brain*. We must all feed and nourish our education system to the best of our ability.

After all, our children are our future.

#3: Rural Medical Care

Access to quality medical care in Rural America has always been a challenge. We simply do not have the collective population to financially support all that is required by the medical services industry. If you are a community that has a small regional hospital, then consider yourself fortunate. Of all of the industries that I have seen suffer throughout my three decades of research, it has been the loss of medical services that has been the most significant blow. Even in communities that are thriving in other ways, it has been hard to preserve or grow access to quality medical care.

However, with technological advancements in the industry, and the consolidation of major medical providers, it is now easier than ever to access care for your community. Video conferencing, telehealth programs, digital doctor's appointments, mobile equipment and testing, online pharmacy services, etc., have given Rural America access to medical care that, only a short decade ago, we were struggling with. The pandemic forced our communities to be more creative, to build more partnerships with regional medical providers, and to aggressively learn how to access virtual medical care.

While your citizens may still have to travel to the nearest metro area to access surgical care and specific disease treatments, we have more access to medical maintenance services than ever before. If your community is not taking advantage of this, I urge the economic development team and/or the city to become involved in building the services. The sustainability and growth of your community depends on it.

#4: Reliable Connectivity

Finally, we must be connected to the outside world. Two of the basic needs we just discussed are completely dependent on access to reliable and high-speed internet throughout the community.

You might ask: What is the difference between Wi-Fi, broadband, and the internet?

Wi-Fi is a local connection, while the Internet is a global one. Wi-Fi is like having an invisible cable connect your device to your router, which then connects you to the Internet.

Broadband refers to the technology used to connect you to the Internet. Remember when you had to dial into the Internet, and only one person could use the line at a time? That was before broadband technology.

Broadband has a wider bandwidth, allowing multiple signals to be transmitted simultaneously. It can use different types of connections, including fiber optic and copper cabling.

The Internet is a massive network of computers, servers, and other devices. The term "World Wide Web"(www.) describes it well: a vast web of interconnected devices spanning the globe.

There you go—a quick lesson in the basics of connectivity. Most citizens assume these things are all the same, but they're not. Admittedly, most don't care, as long as the streaming services on their 70" big-screen TVs work—or heaven forbid someone's phone can't access TikTok or Instagram.

To maintain and grow our communities, we must offer reliable connectivity. City services, utilities, businesses and industries, school systems, medical facilities, emergency management, first responders, and remote workers all depend on it. You simply will not be a community of choice without dependable connectivity. Again, it is not the responsibility of the city or the economic development committee to provide it, but it is essential to assess how well your city is meeting this basic need for growth and sustainability. If it's lacking, what can you do to improve it? It may not be your direct responsibility to provide connectivity, but it is your responsibility to ensure it is available to your community. You simply cannot thrive without it.

There are abundant resources and strategies available to address the need for reliable connectivity. There's no excuse for this to be the issue that holds your community back. A huge shout-out to Electric Cooperatives for taking the lead in aggressively expanding broadband throughout Rural America. They, along with other public and private partners, have made the necessary investments in infrastructure to keep our communities connected—giving them the ability to survive and thrive.

Okay, I admit—it's much more fun and engaging to work on other community factors. But please, pay attention to these four basic needs in order to build a strong foundation for growth.

Ignoring them won't make the problems go away.

Caveat: If you asked me what I believe the next most important basic needs are, I would say adequately maintained infrastructure and a viable downtown. I would like to add a short thought about the importance of maintaining adequate infrastructure—which usually falls under the purview of the city administration and council, along with the county leadership, to address.

Take a long, hard look at the status of your infrastructure: water, roads, utilities, plumbing, etc. People are serious about having safe running water to drink, consistently flushing toilets, roads that don't cause perpetual tire issues, and reliable utilities to plug in that high-definition TV, fancy coffee pot, and flat iron.

Infrastructure is critical because (1) it's expensive to add or replace, (2) it's largely invisible, and (3) it only gets attention when it's failing. And when it fails, it triggers a never-ending cycle of short-term fixes, budget delays—"We'll put it in next year's budget"—or drains your reserves just to patch things up.

The most sustainable communities prioritize infrastructure maintenance each year. It's not flashy or glamorous, but everyone wants to flush their toilets.

And Lord knows that people need their coffee.

Seriously.

A FRESH APPROACH...

DO IT FOR YOU,
not someone new

THIS TOPIC RESIDES VERY DEEP in my heart. As I work in city after city, I often hear EDC boards, city councils, county commissioners, chambers, and committees talk about their future plans in the context of doing it for new residents, coaches, teachers, preachers, new industries, tourists, investors, etc.

I get it. You want to put on your Sunday best and give a good impression to the guests.

But the one phrase I almost never hear used in their dissertation of why they are doing economic development initiatives?

"Let's do it for us."

I rarely hear this.

"Let's do it for us."

Repeat: *I rarely hear this.*

And I mean, in three decades, I have hardly ever heard this.

Come on folks—let's do it for the people who live here. Pay taxes here. Put their kids in school here. Sit on boards here. Go to churches here. Support the non-profits here. Run the businesses here. Buy goods from local merchants here. Support the fire department here.

Can you develop initiatives and marketing that will attract new dollars, new residents, new shoppers and new businesses? Of course you can, and you should.

However, I beg you to shift your mindset away from doing it "for" someone else and instead do it for *you*. Do it for the ones who are already invested in the community—the ones who have remained there through good times and bad—the ones who want a better future for their children, better jobs for themselves and future generations, and who are already stretched thin to pay taxes for city services and safety.

Economic Development involves many aspects, including building the community's infrastructure, creating business opportunities, supporting housing initiatives, increasing the tax base, and marketing your assets to the outside world.

Just remember, you hold the cards. You have the power. You hold the destiny of your community in your hands.

When you work hard to grow your community, do it for your existing citizens. And the rest will come.

It's your community.

Do it for *you*.

And then invite everyone else to join you for the ride.

TAKE A HARD LOOK
in the mirror

IT IS VERY EASY FOR US to fall into the trap of "I wish we were like that community," or "Why do they have that business, and we don't?" or "Why are they growing and we aren't?"

First, remember that cities don't grow or decline overnight. Sometimes, it is so gradual that you hardly realize it's happening, especially if there is no organized effort to help them grow or sustain their population.

Over the past several decades, I've seen several scenarios that can lead to or prevent a decline in cities:

1. A city declines in population due to attrition and non-activity.
2. Businesses leave or close due to a decline in population and non-activity.
3. Schools consolidate with a neighboring community because of a decline in population and non-activity.
4. A city declines in population due to drastic changes in the national economy or specific industries.
5. A city declines in population due to unfortunate natural disasters.
6. A city's population remains steady because of efforts to support local businesses.
7. A city's population remains steady because of organic growth (growth through no specific efforts).
8. A city's population grows because of organized efforts to expand commerce, opportunities, and basic needs.

9. A city's population grows because of organized efforts in the region to collaborate and pursue economic growth together.

With that said, I can tell you that I've never known of a community that did nothing and yet nothing changed. Ever.

As Giuseppe Tomasi do Lampedusa said in his novel *The Leopard*, "If we want things to stay as they are, things will have to change."

It's naïve to think that doing nothing will maintain the status quo. Math and metrics simply do not allow that to happen.

But the harder question is, "How do we start?"

I've heard all of the excuses:
- We don't have any money.
- We don't have anyone who will work on it.
- We are already spread too thin.
- We don't have anyone who is trained to do economic development.
- We don't even know where to start.

I will always contend that economic development — in any population — is not rocket science. It's the pursuit of economic growth and prosperity for a designated area through job creation, capital investment, improved quality of life, and the reliability of basic needs. If you ask 20 seasoned, professional economic developers how to achieve success, they will have 20 different approaches to the challenge. There is no right or wrong way to get from Point A to Point B. But all 20 of them will have one thing in common. They will agree that you have to move beyond talking and start by taking action.

You do have to initiate the hard conversation of "Who do you want to be?" What is the personality and character of your community? What other communities would you aspire to be like?

Here are some quick questions to ask yourself (as a community or a group of stakeholders) that will help you clarify this. These are not hard questions. Please don't overthink them, and just provide short answers.

1. Are we a bedroom community? Or a stand-alone rural community?
2. How many miles are we from the closest international airport?

3. How many miles are we from higher education or vocational and technical training facilities?

4. Do we have assets or a business base that could attract tourism?

5. Do we have any natural resources that can be promoted?

6. Are we located on any state highways or interstates?

7. Do we have rail access to our community?

8. What are our primary and secondary sources of jobs?

9. Is our industry base healthy or hurting?

10. How is our infrastructure holding up? Maintained? Tired? Faulty? New?

11. Is our population growing? Sliding? Holding steady?

12. Do we want to expand our population or maintain our population?

13. What is the condition of our downtown? Good? Bad? Ugly?

14. Do we have any programs in place to assist businesses (new or old)?

15. Is anyone marketing the community to the outside world?

16. Is anyone marketing the community internally?

17. Do we have a database of existing businesses? Available sites?

18. What is special about us? What makes us different from our neighbors?

19. If you were to describe your community in three adjectives, what would they be?

20. Do you have a minimum of medical services in the community?

21. Does your city have a reliable internet service provider?

22. Do we have an inventory of affordable or adequate housing? Who is keeping track?

23. Do you have anyone in the community who is tasked with economic development efforts?

This is the beginning of your conversation moving forward. These questions are intentionally phrased in order to provoke thought and discover three things:

1. Where are you in the process?
2. Are you aware of your assets?
3. Is there a coalition of citizens that can create a realistic vision for the community to rally around?

Regardless of where you are in the pursuit of economic development, please know that you *must* do something. Doing nothing will quickly (or slowly) lead to decline. It's never too late to change course.

I have never seen a community (and I have seen thousands) that did *not* have assets, redeeming qualities, or hidden opportunities. Even in communities that seem to be gasping for their last breath, I can see potential—nuggets of something to build on, glimmers of something special.

It is never too late. And if you are reading this book, I believe you know that you have a special community worth fighting for.

But economic development is hard. It takes guts, resources, intention, and fortitude. I've seen one person turn a community around. I've seen entire communities band together to successfully revitalize their town. And I've seen communities fail—not because of a lack of opportunity, but because of apathy, despair, or an "it's not my job" attitude.

But I have *never* seen a community fail at turning around its destiny when it operates with intention, integrity, enthusiasm, and account-ability. There's a role for everyone.

Just. Do. Something.

I believe in you!

ACCEPTING HELP
is okay

I HAVE HAD THE PRIVILEGE of traveling much of the U.S. by car, giving me the opportunity to see an abundance of rural communities along the way. While I enjoy witnessing the vibrancy of thriving towns, I also find myself drawn to struggling communities, looking for the good.

For over a decade, my husband and I maintained two homes—nine hours apart, driveway to driveway. We are both from the Texas Panhandle but are now empty-nesters in the Austin, Texas, region. While there are a couple of different routes we could take to make the trip back and forth, we mostly stick to one—it's the easiest and most predictable. Since I have been making business trips to Austin for my entire career, there is one city along this route that I have been driving through and observing for more than three decades. It is a struggling little community that began declining in the 1980s and has seen a subtle but consistent slide ever since.

Every single time I drive through this town—well over 500 times by now—I look at it with fresh eyes. It's what I call a "look away" town. A place that does nothing to capture your attention in a positive way, so people just drive through rather than dwell on what they do see—substandard properties, junk cars, overgrown yards, broken curbs and gutters, dilapidated buildings, worn-out signs…you get the picture. It breaks my heart. But the town still has a population, it sits on a highway, and it has a few operating businesses. There's something about it that draws me in. I wonder who lives there, who works there, its history, and what keeps it going.

When I opened my consulting firm, I reached out to them. I told them that I drive through their city regularly and see so much potential. I offered to work with them to create a plan that would help them take baby steps toward revitalization. I was positive and enthusiastic, explaining that I was willing to do it pro bono to help them get started. I listed their many assets—location, highway access, heritage, surrounding growth, and more.

They turned me down. They were offended. They said they weren't a charity case.

I was heartbroken. I apologized and explained that I simply wanted to share my knowledge and that I help communities with projects all over the country.

A few years later, I noticed they had new leadership, so I reached out again—this time with a different approach.

They turned me down again.

This time, their reasons weren't as harsh. They said they simply didn't have the people or resources to do anything, even if the plan itself was free. I understood. Sometimes a project feels so daunting that you don't even know where to start—or who should start.

I didn't give up. Instead, I started sending them case studies the old-fashioned way—by snail mail. One idea at a time. Resources for clean-up initiatives, creative ways to repurpose an empty gas station, programs that could help fund infrastructure improvements, examples of how other communities have revitalized their downtowns, sample ordinances and policies for addressing junk, debris, and easements.

They have never acknowledged receiving these "helpful hints," and that's fine. What makes my heart sing is that now, when I drive through this town, I see baby steps toward improvement. Slowly but steadily, they are making small changes. The average passerby might not notice it yet, but I can definitely see it.

So now, instead of just dropping them a monthly dose of ideas and resources, I now also send a handwritten note to the city of the little things that I noticed on my last drive through their community: the fresh sign, the cleaned windows, the removal of debris, the new sidewalk. I want them to know that their efforts are noticed and appreciated. I don't know who is getting my mail, but I want them to know that what they are doing is important. And it's making a difference. I hope their residents are noticing their efforts. More importantly, I hope it is the residents who are involved and taking the destiny of their city in their hands. Because underneath the tired façade of this little town, I see beauty, history, and opportunity.

They weren't ready for me. And that's okay.

I'm a lot. I know that.

I'm not everyone's cup of tea. I get that, too.

So maybe their path to growth and revitalization is taking a little longer, and that's okay.

But I hope that my encouragement makes a difference, even if it's just to the one person opening the mail that day. Their city is worth saving. And their efforts have been noticed.

I can't wait to drive through and see what's happening next.

Forward progress is contagious.

Keep. Going.

REFRAMING
your attitude

IT ALL COMES DOWN TO ATTITUDE. This one is simple: To have a growing community filled with opportunities for all, thriving businesses, affordable housing and strong infrastructure...you have to want it. You have to *want* it. And work at it. In my research, there are many tangible factors that can dictate whether a community grows or declines in population. There are many reasons a community can grow, including regional industry growth, strategic geographic location, strong organizational efforts, and effective marketing.

All of these factors are measurable. It's the intangibles that are harder to pinpoint. But almost all of the soft reasons a city grows or declines are based on attitude—the attitude of the leadership, the attitude of the residents, and the attitude of the business community. If industry attraction or closures occur, if the overall economic condition improves or declines, or if a community is considered "healthy" or not, it all comes down to attitude.

I can't begin to tell you how many prospects I have taken to visit communities that were perfectly matched on paper. It should have been a slam dunk for the community. But the attitude of the community clearly came through during the visit. Skepticism, distrust, lack of enthusiasm, lack of organization, lack of cohesive talking points, lack of vision, and the dreaded "We don't want change" sentiment were obvious. If there is even a hint of negativity about the community, its people, or its future, it will shine through like a flashing neon light. And the discussion will be over.

There are more than 17,000 communities in the U.S. with populations of 10,000 or less. This is your competition for residents, teachers, police officers, first responders, medical caregivers, small business owners, retailers, industry and service providers. You are not the only game in town.

It is imperative that everyone embrace a shared vision for the growth of the community—one that achieves two key goals: (1) preserving the personality, character, heritage, and history of the city or county, while also (2) positioning it for new and expanded business, entrepreneurship, state-of-the-art education, strong infrastructure, accessible housing, and quality medical care.

You have to give them something to care about. Listen to what they want. Work together to achieve it. Big things and small things. You must give them a reason to care. That's all. Not a tall order. ☺

If you let apathy take over and the citizens stop caring, the slide into decline is not slow. The only good thing about apathy is that it's not permanent. It can be reversed.

Lesson Learned: Communities that grow and thrive do not do it by accident. It doesn't happen overnight through osmosis. If you love your community, show it. If you don't love your community, take steps to fix the issues through positive action. The best way to make sure everyone is on the same page is to keep the channels of communication open, keep the visionary discussions going, practice your message, strengthen your marketing, and BELIEVE IT. When I ask someone, anyone, why they love where they live, and they can tell me without hesitation or negativity, then I know that there is some magic to work with.

If you don't love where you live, then what will it take to get it there? If you can't articulate your issues with the community, then you are not contributing to the solution, you are part of the apathetic reality. Think about it. I mean *really* think about it.

You have a great community with immeasurable potential.

What are you going to do with that gift?

REIMAGINE
your community

FINDING THE BALANCE between what your community "was" and what it "can be" is often tricky, emotional, and nuanced. There is no doubt that every community was built with hard work, with heart, with sacrifice, and with pride. Most of our cities throughout our country are well over a century old, with many decades older than that. There is so much history, so much heritage, so much sentimentality wrapped up in our cities that it is often difficult for citizens to create a new, fresh vision for growth and prosperity.

Many in our leadership positions are second-, third-, or fourth-generation citizens of the community. They have fond memories of a vibrant childhood, of raising their young families in the community, of spending time with grandparents and neighbors. They fondly remember the community during a time of vibrancy and economic prosperity.

But time can be a harsh reminder of what happens when we don't tend to the garden. Our cities are like gardens. We need to establish their boundaries, till the soil, fertilize regularly, plant the seeds of the community's choice, water them, nurture them, harvest them, and celebrate them. It's a constant cycle of planting, sowing, nurturing, and celebrating. If we don't tend to them, weeds can outgrow the plants and overrun the boundaries. Weeds can choke out the sun, steal the water, knock down barriers, and overtake the garden.

Like gardens, our communities need constant nurturing, watering, weeding, and fertilizing. You get to choose what you plant in your garden.

Flowers? Fruits? Vegetables? Wildflowers? Herbs? Shrubs? Nuts? Christmas trees? The options are endless. But you must also consider the soil, the environment, access to sun and water, proximity to other gardens, weather patterns, special needs of the chosen crops, and desired outcomes. In your communities, you need to do the same—determine what kind of community you want, plan it, plant it, nurture it, water it, fertilize it, and enjoy it.

Now that we have this scenario in mind, let's think about how you can "reimagine" what your community can be. Perhaps, decades ago, it was a strong agricultural community, but now renewable energy and state-of-the-art farming technology have emerged. Perhaps decades ago, you had a bustling business district, but now an interstate was built one mile away, and people bypass your community. Perhaps decades ago, your city had a vibrant and active downtown area that served as the heartbeat of the city.

But now, with aging historical buildings in need of renovation and attention, new businesses have located elsewhere. There are a number of reasons why cities change over time. The important point here is that it is possible to "honor your history but build for your future."

There is a way to preserve what makes your community special—the history, the culture, the character. And you may feel very sentimental about many of your aging businesses and buildings. But to grow or, at the very least, remain a healthy and vibrant community, it is critical to look at your city with fresh eyes. We will talk about windshield tours in another chapter, but it is important to remember that the most dynamic communities are those that are intentional with their growth, have incorporated new and exciting businesses, and have found innovative ways to honor their history and culture. You *can* have the best of both worlds.

However, your community must make adjustments to stay relevant to new generations and add additional services to stay relevant to older generations. Your city today is not the same as it was in 1895, 1925, 1975, or even 2015. It's exciting to talk about the tweaks a community can make to provide a dynamic, affordable, and memorable quality of life.

Just as your wardrobe has changed over the decades, so should your city.

Let's all admit that we love a beautiful garden. Look at your city with fresh eyes and reimagine what it "can" be.

You are only limited by your imagination.

Ideas to Consider:
- Keep a list of aspirational cities that offer services, businesses, or assets that you enjoy. This is easily done when you are traveling on business, choosing a destination for holidays and vacation or visiting friends and family. What did you love about the destination? Accommodations? Recreation? The vibe? Events? Shops? Restaurants? Nightlife? Lifestyle? Aesthetics? History? Arts? Take notes and take pictures. They will become important examples when having discussions about where and how to allocate your community's resources.
- Create a digital vision board for memorable things that you have seen: a renovated building, cool signage, memorable landscaping, streetscapes, lighting, benches, public parks, public restroom facilities, sports fields and complexes, renovated movie theaters, town squares, parking lots, vintage motels and gas stations, billboards, etc. It's hard to verbally explain to others the potential you can see in your community, but much easier to show them what is possible. Visuals are your best strategy to gather enthusiasm and engagement for local improvements.

Consider this Assignment:

In the spring, ask the members of your EDC board, the city council, the chamber board, and volunteers from the community to spend the next six months snapping photos of things they like when they are visiting other communities to shop, obtain medical care, vacation, business trips, etc. Ask each of them to submit their ten favorite photos in early fall. Categorize the photos into a slide presentation (housing, hotels, restaurants, parks, stadiums, welcome signage, industrial parks, business signage, lighting, sidewalks, renovated buildings, tourist attractions, recreation, etc.). I believe you'll be surprised by the commonalities among the photos and the volume of similar images.

Every time we do this exercise, priorities always naturally rise to the top, some dynamic new ideas emerge, and people get excited about what "can" be. Visualization is a method that cannot be underestimated.

One of my recent client cities did this exercise, and almost half of the participants turned in photos of overpasses.

Yep, you heard me.

Overpasses.

Who knew it was even a topic that inspired passion? While they ultimately did not emulate any of the overpasses they saw, it identified that this was a priority to many in the community. They had engineers create renditions of what they did want, and then they began to work with their state Department of Transportation to implement a new landscaped overpass at the entrance to their community.

People take millions of photos on their phones, so getting participation should not be an issue as long as they know the end game. It will allow the stakeholders to see what is an attraction to others and will open their imaginations to what "can" be.

Be who you are. Only better.

REPURPOSING
when possible

I REMEMBER WHEN MY MOM used to take me downtown to the Tot Shop. It was a children's boutique and our go-to destination when looking for that special Easter or Picture Day outfit. We didn't shop there often, but it was always a treat when we did. On the opposite corner was the fire station. Across the street was a Ben Franklin store, a furniture store, and C.R. Anthony's.

On the next block was a western store, the bus station/soda shop, and a bank. On the next block was the Merle Norman makeup store, a jewelry store, and the LaRita Theater. On the next block was the flower shop, the Mission Twin Theater, and the newspaper office. On the next block was the Dallam County Courthouse and Library.

You see where I'm going with this, right?

I have fond memories of those downtown excursions. They were memorable and fun. As I got older, my friends and I used to ride our bikes downtown to get treats from the bus station or buy snacks from the Ben Franklin store.

Fast-forward 50 years: That building at the end of the block in downtown Dalhart, Texas, has housed more stores than I can count. It's amazing that I can't always remember my last address, but I can remember those stores from 50 years ago.

The point is, don't let your fond memories of "what was" get in the way of "what can be."

I still love going to downtown Dalhart, where they still have the original brick streets and beautiful big trees. But other than the LaRita

Theater, the bank, the courthouse square, and the museum, the other stores and buildings have changed types and ownership many, many times over.

It was sad for everyone when the Mission Twin Theaters closed down, and it took years before someone reopened a different business on the premises. It was hard to picture it as anything but what it had been in our childhood memories. How could it possibly be a church? Or a community center? How could the old bus station become a high-end furniture store? How could a Western store become a coffee shop and bookstore? How could an old post office become private corporate offices? It's hard to fathom, but it is necessary to open your mind to repurposing buildings for more relevant uses in today's world.

I don't have the same needs, desires, or budget that I had when I was 12 years old. People want ten different coffee options now, instead of just regular or decaf. The bus stations have moved out to the highways for easier access. People aren't just looking for books in bookstores anymore; they are remote working, drinking coffee, and staying for a while. They want Wi-Fi and comfy chairs, whether they buy anything or not.

Look at your community with fresh eyes. What do you have, and what do you need? You have an older hotel, but a new hotel just opened on the edge of town. You need housing for railroad workers and harvest crews. Consider turning the old hotel into efficiency, studio, or extended-stay apartments. You have an old historic theater that can't compete with the new eight-screen multiplexes in the city 30 miles away. Consider renovating it and turning it into a children's art and theater center or a community auditorium for music, recitals, plays, melodramas, concerts, candidate forums, business programs, and more.

Our cities are aging, and so are our buildings. I understand and believe that when a building has declined to the point of being a danger, it should be removed and replaced with something more relevant. But always as a *last* resort. I love the character of our historic buildings. I'm never in favor of tearing down an old and historic building just because it is tired and in need of renovations.

Of course, many factors come into play when bringing an old building back to life—overpriced value by the owner, daunting renovations to bring it up to code, ADA requirements, and more—but it *can* be done, and done fabulously. And I'm not just talking about downtown buildings.

I've seen old courthouses turned into beautiful shopping and restaurant centers.

I've seen old implement stores transformed into breweries and distilleries.

I've seen old gas stations repurposed into professional offices, ice cream shops, wine bars, visitor centers, and boutiques.

I've seen second and third floors of buildings turned into Airbnbs, apartments, offices, conference centers, and specialty shops.

I've seen old high schools converted into family entertainment and shopping centers.

I've seen old malls transformed into high-tech training centers and business incubators.

I've seen silos turned into offices and rail cars converted into hotels.

I could go on and on. I'm so impressed with the ingenuity of our rural entrepreneurs who see beyond what a building was in a previous era and bring it back to life with a new purpose. You will hear me say this over and over again...

You *can* honor your history and build for the future.

It's possible.

Package those wonderful childhood memories and file them away. Then, open your mind to all the new potential uses for your existing buildings and sites. Even better, make a list of needs and wants. Then, make a list of existing and available properties (regardless of condition) and have a *crazy* discussion about each one to see if there is a potential match. Yes, that old tire shop can become an antique store. Yes, that old bank can become a senior center. Yes, that old gun shop can become a pharmacy. And yes, that old barn can become a steakhouse.

You are only limited by your imagination.

I'm not naïve—sometimes, we do need a new building. Some are simply in too serious a state of disrepair. But I encourage you to truly analyze the condition and availability of every building and every commercial site in your community so that when you are arranging site visits for potential industries, entrepreneurs, and investors, you have a variety of options to share.

The downtown Dalhart of 2025 does not resemble the downtown Dalhart of 1975, but it is still filled with dynamic businesses and commerce intent on helping you make new memories (and new sales). And for the sentimental ones—there will be mementos from the businesses of yesteryear on the walls, allowing you to honor history while enjoying the conveniences of today.

DON'T REINVENT *the wheel*

WE ARE ALL ORIGINALS. And let's face it, we like being different.

In economic development, to be successful in recruitment and business development, you must be different. The competition is simply too fierce to blend in.

But, with that said, it's also smart and efficient to learn from others. Every action plan that I develop for my clients include no less than fifteen to twenty case studies.

Because there is no need to reinvent the wheel.

I know, I know. We don't want to be like someone else. We want to be different, special, and original. I know this, I get this, and I agree with this.

But I also know, from working with and researching hundreds of communities, that your needs, wants, assets, and challenges all have, let's say, 80% of commonality. We all want good homes, great schools, access to medical care, handy commerce, good water, safe streets, fun events… I wish I could tell you that everyone is different, but in reality, we are more the same than not.

Our kids *want* the same things. Our parents *need* the same things.

It's what we do in that 20% that sets us apart. In my work, I've seen a lot of industrial parks, city halls, city parks, splash pads, swimming pools, and sports fields. But I have yet to see two that are exactly alike. I've seen more breweries, restaurants, sports bars, wine bars, and distilleries than I can count (the fun part of my job!). But I have yet to see two that are exactly alike. I've stayed in hundreds of bed & breakfasts, eaten at thousands of burger and BBQ joints, and visited hundreds of chambers of commerce and visitor centers. Yep, no two are alike.

So instead of getting caught up in "I want to be different," take a moment to gather research on a project you'd like to pursue and see how others have successfully achieved it. By using case studies in your research, you can learn both the good and the bad—what to do and what not to do. You'll see what preliminary environmental studies were needed, what permits were required, what skills the labor force needed, the average water and utility use, which programs supported the project, who the partners or collaborators were, the total cost, what they would do differently, the project timeline from start to finish, potential pitfalls, and what kind of market research was conducted. You see? The list goes on and on.

Imagine starting with the answers to all these questions *before* launching your new business or community project. Imagine knowing the hurdles, the opportunities, and the information you didn't even know to ask about. Imagine knowing what to expect and being prepared for it instead of flying by the seat of your pants.

Case studies help you learn, spark new ideas, avoid pitfalls, and be more financially prepared for what lies ahead.

But it's that 20% of the project that makes you different, unique, and special—special location, special menu items, special signage, special amenities, special aesthetics, special customer service, special marketing. That's what will make your project stand out and be memorable.

So unless you are opening a franchise, where everything is required to be the same, don't get hung up on not wanting to "copy" or "study" someone else's project.

It's a smart move, and I promise you…

You will still be different.

REGIONALISM

works

REGIONALISM IS EASILY MY FAVORITE Rural Economic Development Strategy. I've lived it, breathed it, and have seen it work. The concept of "regionalism" is often at odds with the mission and objectives of local economic development organizations. After all, most EDOs are funded locally, and it is only good business sense that your investment in economic development strategies should directly impact your city, county, or territory. Economic development is also competitive; therefore, it is human nature that an EDO would want to focus only on the win for their stakeholders.

But I urge our associates in economic development, especially those in rural communities, to look at the assets and opportunities that exist beyond their immediate and stated boundaries.

Here's why:
- From a **recruitment** standpoint, regardless of the population of your city or county, prospects are interested in more than just the "site." They are looking for a talent pipeline and workforce base that, most likely, will come from a commuting area beyond your city limits or county lines. They are looking at nearby training facilities, diverse housing options, and a variety of recreational and cultural offerings. In many cases, they are searching for a large market for their product or services. I promise you, they are not looking at your boundaries, only you are.

- From an **expanding business** standpoint, many of the same issues listed above also apply. If your existing industries have the potential to grow, their current location may not have the ability to offer everything the company needs, including additional talent, skilled labor, workforce training, housing, and more. They are considering the infrastructure to get their goods in or out of their facility, the ability to attract a consistent workforce and the strategies to build a consumer market far beyond their city. Their planning does not include a stop at the city limits. To keep them and help them grow, you will need to think beyond your city limits, too.
- From a **start-up's** point of view, many times, their market knows no boundaries to start with. While they may be focusing locally to build their customer base, they know that future growth will depend on expanding their brand, their promotions, their service or product offerings far beyond their city limits.

In a global market that has such an array of technology available for promotion, production, delivery and services, the days of recruiting, growing and protecting the treasures of economic growth in our own backyards are over.

From the smallest of cities to the largest of urban areas, prospects are no longer interested in boundaries. They acknowledge that the incentives included in proposals may be tied to specific locations, but they have also indicated that the best and most attractive opportunities are those that include support from a regional level. They want to know that there is open communication between neighboring cities. They want reassurance that a workforce from an entire area can be depended on. They want to be able to assure their employees that their lifestyle needs are available nearby.

I know it's incredibly hard for economic development practitioners to focus on regional initiatives if their boards and councils do not understand the needs or benefits. But you can't be everything to everybody. If you don't have an international airport, chances are, you aren't going to get one now. If you don't have an abundance of water, a miraculous source of water is probably not in the cards. If you don't have interstate access, that may not happen in your lifetime. But that doesn't mean that you can't broaden your scope to include the assets that your neighbors have. Or that your neighbors can't do the same. It's a win/win for all.

Synergy: syn-er-gy

the interaction or cooperation of two or more organizations, substances, or other agents to produce a combined effect greater than the sum of their separate effects.

Forget the football rivalries. We live in a global economy. From the smallest of projects to the rare and unusually large opportunities, the benefits of expanding your thinking beyond your immediate boundaries far outweigh the cost. The collateral value of regionalism can also include the following:

1. Leveraged resources
2. Bigger voice on policy issues
3. Larger & more competitive footprint to attract attention
4. Diverse perspectives for regional growth strategies
5. Enhanced marketing that complements the local efforts

Yes, economic development has been and will remain a competitive industry. But when you and your neighboring cities agree that what's good for them is good for you (and vice versa), then that's when the magic happens.

Case in point: In 2005, Hilmar Cheese was looking for a location for a new state-of-the-art cheese & whey manufacturing facility. Amarillo, Texas, knew that they did not meet the criteria. Dalhart, Texas, knew that they had a very competitive site that met the criteria, but did not have the construction & engineering sources, the milk production, or the workforce & training pipeline to support the RFP. The Amarillo EDC voted to financially incentivize the proposal based in Dalhart, located two counties and 85 miles away (much to the consternation of their citizens).

Stratford, Dumas, Texline, Gruver, Sunray, Spearman, Channing, Hartley, Vega, Hereford and many other Texas cities supported the proposal with the promise of housing, workforce, milk production, and ancillary services to the proposed plant.

The cities of Clayton and Tucumcari, New Mexico, Guymon, Oklahoma, and cities in southeast Colorado and southwest Kansas were also important cities that came into play when the parent company was making the decision of where to locate their next plant. Several states were considered, but it was the overwhelming commitment to regionalism that tilted the decision to locate the plant in Dalhart, Texas.

For those who questioned the financial commitment of the Amarillo EDC to provide actual dollars to the project, their ROI turned out to be more than tenfold in direct impact (i.e., actual $$$) on the construction, engineering, supplies, and labor provided by Amarillo-based companies. But more importantly, the Amarillo EDC knew that by locating a game-changing industry in the region, they would be the beneficiary of the supply chain companies that would want to locate near the plant, but needed a more metropolitan area. This visionary action proved to be true.

In addition, Hilmar Cheese has completed more than three expansions since their location in the Texas Panhandle, which continues to benefit everyone located within 200 miles of the plant.

Sidenote: More than 15 cities in the region (and almost all of the cities mentioned above) submitted site proposals to the company at the beginning of the process. They all worked extremely hard to locate the project in *their* city. However, once the shortlist was announced… they all chose to embrace the opportunities that the project would bring to the region rather than wallow in the bitterness of defeat.

Collaboration: col-lab-o-ra-tion

the action of working with someone to produce or create something of mutual benefit.

This is not an unusual scenario. It has happened all over the country. Successful regional initiatives are a common denominator in areas of economic growth. I am inspired by the many vibrant and dynamic regional economic development organizations that currently exist and are achieving great things for their collective stakeholders. (I have studied almost all of them.)

If you are not part of a regional economic development effort, I encourage you to join one. If your region does not have an organized regional initiative, then start one. It's not as easy as I'm making it sound, but it is certainly worth it. I know a lot of people who can help you. Your regional involvement does not replace your local objectives; however, it can greatly complement, compound, and leverage your development efforts.

Let's all think beyond our boundaries. Find ways to work together. True economic development cannot happen in a silo.

As a kid, did you want to play in the sandbox by yourself, or join the one in which all of the kids were gathered and having a good time? It's a big sandbox and there's room for everyone who wants to play.

Let's go!

ARTICULATE *the end game*

HAVING AN "END GAME" for economic development initiatives is critical to gaining the trust of your community leaders and citizens. Although efforts are most often ongoing, benchmarks, objectives, timelines, costs, responsibilities, and benefits are important to the program's sustainability.

The most important question your community stakeholders can ask themselves is, "What does economic development success look like to me? Is it jobs? Is it new small businesses? Is it housing? Is it a population increase? Is it receiving grants for improvements? Is it downtown revitalization? What is it?"

I can sadly report that many strong economic developers or economic development boards have found themselves in the quandary of "mixed message expectations"—or worse, no stated expectations. What if they were successful in attracting new business and creating new jobs, but the expectation of the community was to revitalize the downtown or clean up the highway blight? What if they were successful in creating a foundation of small business and entrepreneurship programs for the community, but the leadership wanted them to build relationships with developers for housing? What if they created fabulous new marketing materials, built a strong social media presence, and put the city on the map for tourism, but the citizens wanted a new swimming pool or sports complex?

Do you get where I'm going here?

Yes, most communities would be happy with any improvements, any growth—anything new. But you can see now that in the absence of articulating the end game, you are leaving a lot of gray area for miscommunication, missteps, misunderstandings, and perceived missed opportunities. Many communities would have those things on their goals list, but are they spelled out in an action plan as priorities? Is the end game clear? I have seen way too many good economic developers get fired for creating jobs instead of cleaning up blight, or creating housing instead of a community center, or fixing up the downtown instead of filling up the industrial park. It's a shame, but it happens more than we care to admit.

We can do a couple of things to avoid the "either/or" conundrum:
1. Establish a clear understanding of expectations of the economic development efforts, noting the duties that are specific to the EDC, those that are specific to the City, those that are specific to the Main Street Program, and those that are performed for the greater good of the community.
2. Establish a budget that correlates with the marketing, travel, memberships, prospect engagement, and other objectives listed in your action plan and other initiatives as they may arise.
3. Establish a process for handling prospects and involve the EDC board or committee in said process. Examples of prospect processes can be provided on request.
4. Establish a process of benchmarking to measure the success of initiatives, results of marketing campaigns, and growth in the community. Sales tax collections, building and home permits, water hook-ups, workforce numbers, school enrollment etc. can all be benchmarked to measure growth.
5. Establish a process of how you will reach out and maintain communications and engagement with your existing businesses.

Develop a process of announcing your economic development plans and initiatives to the community. This will drive engagement, support, and participation. While negotiations with companies, financial reviews, background checks, etc., should remain confidential, it is still important to provide the community with overall plans, strategies, initiatives, and programs. They may become entrepreneurs, ambassadors, volunteers, etc. Transparency of goals and initiatives is critical to community engagement and support.

And most importantly, have a complete understanding of what "successful economic development" means to the community. It's going to be different things to different people—all of our personal priorities are different. So by developing and publicly saying, "This is what we are working on: this is the end game," you can alleviate much of the drama of, "Why aren't you doing this for me?"

Most of all, they can't help you if they don't know what is going on. I believe you'll find that most citizens are interested and want to be instrumental in the future growth of their community in some way. After all, they are already taxpayers, investors, and believers in the community.

Invite them along for the journey.

As they say, the more the merrier.

COLLABORATION *& leverage*

COLLABORATION IS CRITICAL. It is also the hardest. We are all wired to be singularly focused on our own tasks at hand, primarily the objectives of *our* organization and *our* mission. In fact, in today's fast-paced business world, it seems that is all we would ever have time for. In short, it is simply not sustainable to pursue economic growth alone.

All communities have economic strengths and weaknesses, but successful ones share a common characteristic that eludes the unsuccessful: They are able to work with other organizations to pursue a common vision for their community. They recognize that one person, one board, one effort cannot achieve and sustain a high level of community vibrancy alone. It takes everyone being successful in their own lanes, but driving in the same direction.

The ones who are missing the boat are the communities that are so focused on their own agenda that they miss the opportunity to expand their support and their access to expertise and funding.

Collaboration is a buzzword these days. But for decades I have seen it work. The development of partnerships, shared visions, and shared funding is not a fly-by-night feel-good function. It's for real. I've watched communities grow over the decades, because of collaboration.

Imagine one organization coordinating an event to showcase their donors and thank their supporters—funded by a partnering organization that invites out-of-town prospects to attend and learn more about the community.

Imagine a hospital district benefiting from a mobile medical unit, funded by a consortium of local companies, designed to serve as a mobile blood collection unit, provide mammograms, and offer basic cardiac tests, blood pressure readings, and blood sugar tests at the workplace.

Imagine a local industry offering programs at the high school to explain the skills needed at their plant.

These are all examples of collaboration—true "win/win" scenarios for everyone involved. Always look for partners. It will make the effort more expansive, more rewarding, and more productive.

And maybe, as a side effect, more fun.

Lesson Learned: Some communities have attempted to break down conflicts and build collaborative efforts but have failed. Though it appears to be intuitive and easy to make cooperation happen, it is actually very difficult. Getting an economic development organization, a city, a county, a school ISD, a hospital district, a chamber, and industry to all agree and pursue a common outcome is tricky, but definitely possible. The most familiar roadblock is who gets credit for successes. Communities that have achieved economic development successes know that success generates enough credit that all functions can share equally and collaborate for the best interest of the community.

YOU ARE
special

IT'S NECESSARY TO BE DIFFERENT to be competitive for new jobs, new industry, and new growth. You must differentiate yourself and articulate what makes you unique from the other thousands of cities of the same population within a multi-state region.

For several decades, I have taught a marketing class for economic development organizations, regional groups, cities, counties and chambers of commerce. An exercise I have used consistently is taking samples of marketing pieces (both print and digital) from all across the U.S. I give a few examples to each table or each participant and ask them to write down five things that they are gleaning from the marketing collateral's message.

I appreciate that everyone is always so earnest in completing this exercise. Then, I ask each table to have a representative (or each individual, in some cases) read out loud their list of message points. I can almost tell you in advance what most of them will say: good schools, good people, good location, good quality of life… the perfect place to live, work and play… yada yada yada. You get it. After the third table said the same thing, they got the message, too.

The photos, colors, and fonts may be different, but the message was the same.

Outbound economic development marketing is exponentially better now. But for decades, instead of trying hard to stand out, people thought they better make sure everyone knew that they had, at minimum, those things.

I can assure you, no one is considering your community without doing their homework first. Everything anyone wants to know about your community is available out in the digital universe somewhere. But what they may not know are the very things that set you apart. The very things that make you special and different from all of your neighbors.

So what makes you different?

Is it your city's investment in infrastructure? Is it special skills that your existing workforce enjoys? Is it the short commute to recreation? Is it your visionary action plan? Is it your high school's relationship with local employers? Is it your traffic counts? Is it your entrepreneur ecosystem and support? Is it your unique demographics? Is it your distance to an international airport? Is it your pipeline of preferred skilled labor? Is it your technology class offerings? Is it your high percentage of veteran employees and business owners? Is it your supply chain opportunities? Is it your aggressive incentive programs? Is it your utility infrastructure? Whatever that difference is… promote it. You have to get beyond the great schools, great people, great quality of life discussion. That's just not enough.

If your high school offers STEM classes, promote it. If your community has dynamic entrepreneurship programs, promote them. If you have a ten-year plan for housing development, promote it. If you have a new water system that allows for growth over a 25-year span, promote it. If your high school just passed a bond for newly updated amenities, promote it.

Lesson Learned: For years, I have taken prospects on visits to various cities, often in one day or consecutive days. By the end of the trip, they have a hard time differentiating between all of the industrial parks they have seen, the city halls they have been in, and the conversations about incentives they have had. My friends who are realtors have shared with me that they run into the same thing when showing multiple homes to prospective buyers: they all start to merge together.

What the prospects do remember are the small things that make you different. The greeting, the packets, the pre-planning, the flawless execution of the visit, and the enthusiasm. And most of all, the follow-up. Many times, the cities do not know the identity of the companies in advance, but you can tell that they have a tested and efficient system for hosting prospects. In the cases that the city does know their identity, and they really do their homework and know all that they can about the company, there is no excuse not to step it up and make the visit even more memorable.

I recently hosted a prospect company in a city that had learned most of the employees relocating to the new location were hikers. Although the company's primary focus was on available industrial sites, the host city arranged for lunch to be held under a tent in the most popular nearby hiking area. They didn't make a big deal out of it—just casually mentioned that this is where employees could go before or after work, or during lunch. It was a memorable visit, and the company was impressed that the city took the time to learn what would make their employees happy.

On another community visit, the EDC learned that the company's CEO had recently had another child and had just returned from maternity leave. So, in addition to their usual swag, they included some locally branded baby items for her. They didn't call attention to it, and she didn't even notice until she got home. But the quiet gesture made a strong impression.

Finally, on another visit, one EDC knew that the prospect team would be visiting several cities over four days and that theirs was not one of the "stayover" sites. They arranged for a box of welcome snacks to be placed in the bus that picked them up from the airport, along with a branded shipping box that was pre-addressed and ready to be mailed.

This allowed the prospect team to collect information and swag from all the cities, pack it into the box, and have it express-shipped to their office at the sponsoring EDC's expense. It was waiting on their desk when they returned—branded with the city's logo on the outside and a thank-you letter inside. So, while the city didn't have the opportunity to entertain the prospects overnight, they were able to make the **first** impression, the **site visit** impression, and the **final** impression from the trip.

Most of all, if possible, find out dietary preferences/restrictions or cultural considerations in advance. Don't assume every company wants to experience your famous BBQ—they may be vegetarians. Don't assume your prospects would enjoy your renowned chicken-fried steak for lunch—they may be eating three big meals a day on the trip and prefer a salad, wrap, or light sandwich.

On the flip side, they may be excited to try your famous gumbo, steak, or breakfast tacos. Just gather as much information as possible ahead of time and plan accordingly. If advance details are limited, ensure you have a variety of choices available.

I call that frosting. Many bakers create similar cakes, but it's the frosting that sets them apart. But please take note: it's what you say, your prepared materials, your presentation, your team, your talking points, your ability to answer questions, your preparation, and your follow-up that will set you apart from the others.

You don't want to be remembered for what you didn't do, and you also don't want to be forgettable.

Grand gestures are great and definitely memorable, but it's often the small details and the personal touches that make the biggest difference.

PRIMARY JOBS
vs. retail

IN MY ECONOMIC DEVELOPMENT FACILITATION DUTIES over the last three decades, one thing became abundantly clear:

We all want what we don't have.

Regardless of population, we all want what we don't have. My urban clients want a Whole Foods or the latest fancy pickleball court. My rural clients want a Sonic or a craft brewery.

I'm being facetious.

Sort of.

But it's true. The grass is always greener on the other side of the fence.

In Rural America, we are faced with a challenge that our urban neighbors don't necessarily have. We have the chicken and the egg dilemma.

Rural community members want more amenities, more fast food, more retail. But they do not necessarily have the population to support these types of businesses without the help of traffic and some really great marketing to bring dollars in from outside. They want more primary jobs that pay livable wages. But they don't want to live in a community with little or no retail amenities or entertainment.

As a traditional economic developer, I want to scream, "PRIMARY JOBS CREATE ROOFTOPS AND ROOFTOPS CREATE RETAIL OPPORTUNITIES!" My mind and my experience tell me that this is a solid mantra and pretty true in most cases.

But I've been proven wrong in some of these cases, and I'm not afraid to admit it.

I live 90 miles from a rural community that is basically 90% retail. No industry. No commercial businesses. Just a few city or county jobs and a small elementary school. All kids go to a neighboring community for junior high. This community made the intentional decision to go all in on their vision to be mecca for shoppers. They attracted antique stores, holiday stores, boutiques, home goods, discount stores for high-end designers, furniture warehouses, etc.

Once their business base began to grow and people began to arrive, then the restaurants, cabins and Airbnbs followed. They started holding huge shopping weeks twice a year, one in the spring and one in the fall. Then, some stores began to stay open 5 days a week. And then more stores moved in. It is a shopper's heaven. They have done well by sticking with their vision and making it happen.

But I would be remiss if I didn't also caution the following: Without diversifying their economy, they are completely at the mercy of the fluctuations in the economy, many of their vendors are impacted by bad weather, and even the price of fuel could impact their shopping extravaganzas. As long as they are taking precautions for the unexpected, I wish them continued success. I love to visit their little shopping mecca and enjoy taking guests there as well.

On the flip side, I'm also aware of the challenges that a community has with a heavy industrial base. The employees of those companies want a good quality of life for themselves and their families. If they had the opportunity to choose to live there, or commute from a nearby city, then they are going to base their decision on multiple factors: the quality of life, the amenities offered, the shopping, hospitality, and food choices, the excellence of the school system, access to medical care, etc.

People don't automatically live where they work or work where they live anymore. People are more mobile and have more choices of where to reside and where to spend their money.

I still believe that "retail follows rooftops" most of the time. So I'm begging you: Before you invest your life savings in a business endeavor without the appropriate population or market to support it, take a hard, hard look at who your customers are, where they live, and the volume of the potential customer base.

Just because you want a Sonic doesn't mean you have the population to support it. Just because you want a Wendy's doesn't mean you have the traffic to support it. Retail and hospitality chains—whether they are fast food restaurants, home goods, hotels, or retail clothing—don't locate if their extensive market research doesn't show that they are viable locations. They will not invest, nor will they allow a franchiser to invest if the math simply does not work. So instead of being upset with your local economic developer for what they "can't get," do the research to find out what is feasible for your population, your traffic, and your geographic location.

Pursuing and focusing on the development and attraction of primary jobs will provide long-term viability for the community. And once those jobs and a minimum threshold of population growth are in place, the much-awaited retail development will follow. But it doesn't have to be an either/or situation. The fact remains that a community filled with jobs that pay above-average wages and benefits will establish a foundation for sustainability, allowing retail jobs to complement them in a productive way. Primary jobs also provide the much-needed dollars that circulate through the community, supporting other businesses.

The best thing you can do is be patient. Ensure your land is properly zoned, understand your local permitting and regulatory environment, work on improving local business opportunities, provide training for entrepreneurs, prepare marketing campaigns that reflect your quality of life and economic activity, build relationships with regional bankers, brokers, and developers, and grow the community.

One job at a time.

My friends in retail development and attraction are the best. They are pragmatic and will be honest with you about what is a good fit for your community. Being realistic about who you are and where you are is the best strategy of all.

TAKING ACTION...

LOOK WITH *fresh eyes*

I AM A BIG BELIEVER in windshield tours. While it's critical to dig deeper into the internal functions of a community, you've got to admit that it's the exterior that gives you the first impression.

Ask yourself: *Would I want to stop here? Would I want to stay here? Would I want to shop here? Would I want to live here? Would I want to explore further? Would I be proud to live here?*

What kind of impression is your community making?

I have completed windshield tours all across the U.S., and have found interesting commonalities in many of the cities and regions I view.

Someone who has lived in a city for quite some time—usually a decade or more—often views their community through the filter of how it used to be. Our brains default back to a time that was good, vibrant, and active.

Someone new to a community, however, looks at everything. They notice everything. Who lives here? What business is this? Why is this street sign broken? Where is the library? This light is out. When does this store open? Where is the sidewalk ramp?

More importantly, when something is unattractive, instead of really looking at it, people "look away." This is why, in many of my keynotes and workshops, you'll hear me refer to a building, a sign, a site, a park, or a business as a "look-away." It's not that we don't care about it—it's just that there's nothing compelling enough to hold our attention. It's easier to look away and move forward.

This phenomenon can collectively hurt the impression our city makes. Is your city filled with reasons for people to look away? More often than not, this happens due to junk, abandoned cars, broken fences, substandard buildings, old signs, dirty windows, trash, and yes, even faded murals.

First impressions matter. We need to make people want to learn more, to look further, to stop and spend money with local businesses, to want to stay, live, and work in our community.

Over the years, I have learned to document everything I see using my **Windshield Tour Template** (available to you as a bonus by scanning the QR code at the back of this book). Not just in writing. I don't just give it a grade or ranking—I back it up with hundreds of photos and videos that depict what I saw.

For years, there I was, with my little disposable Kodak camera, standing on the corner, taking pictures. Then I graduated to better cameras and better photos. Then to high-definition images with my phone. And now, I take narrated video and present my findings in a professional, edited digital format that can be easily shared among the pertinent organizations in the community.

Windshield tours, if done right, are hard. They are often harsh. It's tough to be the bearer of bad news. To do the best job, it's important to be honest and candid about what I'm seeing. But just as importantly, I make sure to highlight the good things I see as well. Some communities may be going through a hard season, but I can always find assets and opportunities that others might overlook. It's what economic developers do. It's like a sixth sense. But it's how we use it that makes the most impact.

Yes, I'm going to bring to light the weaknesses in a community's visual impression. But I will also follow up with ideas, strategies, and resources to help fix them. No one likes the gloom and doom of bad news, but it can certainly be softened when paired with an exciting initiative that turns a negative view into a positive one. So many things are easily fixed. Everything can be remedied—it's just that sometimes, implementing the right remedy is painful.

I can bet that most cities already have solid ordinances on their books regarding junk cars, abandoned vehicles, storage tanks, fencing requirements, broken windows, safety hazards, fire hazards, and more.

Getting the ordinances on the books is the easy part.

Getting the city to enforce them is a whole other issue.

I'm not criticizing the city or the enforcers. I sympathize with them: It's hard to enforce laws on our neighbors, local businesses, and people who believe deeply in private property rights. I recognize that. However, to attract local commerce and outside investment, everyone must understand that maintaining an attractive community is critically important.

If you turn a blind eye and let a few citizens get away with it, this can start a slide that becomes hard to slow down. Ultimately, you are bound to let everyone get away with it. Where you once had a beautiful, dynamic city, you end up with a tired and messy community. It's not fair to those who want and need a clean, safe, and vibrant city to keep their business afloat. It's not fair to those who spend endless hours maintaining their yards, creating a beautiful impression for visitors. And it's not fair to business owners who maintain their exteriors to a high standard, only to find themselves next door to someone who does not.

The simple answer to this problem is to enforce the ordinances. Treat everyone the same. Take the guesswork and favoritism out of it. Make it clear that there is no gray area. No second, third, or fourth chances. If someone is in violation of an ordinance, give them a warning and 30 days to rectify the issue. If they do not comply, they should be fined, and the city should take action.

They can tow away junk cars and tanks, repair fences, condemn unsafe buildings, shut down businesses lacking fire safety equipment, replace broken lights, and more. Cities also have the ability to place liens on properties to recover the costs of ordinance enforcement. The key is to have strong ordinances in place, ensure all citizens are aware of them, and then enforce them clearly and fairly.

Helpful Tip: Before enforcing ordinances on private citizens, make sure all government-owned property is properly maintained. You need to clean up your own backyard before calling out the neighbors.

However, it's not just about negative property impressions. It's about your city's identity. It takes less than six seconds for someone to decide whether to keep looking at something or to look away. It takes less than

30 seconds for someone to form an impression of a city, a business, a person, or an experience. When you have a clean and welcoming city, you are successfully achieving the following:

- You are giving people a reason to stop and enjoy your community.
- You are giving potential residents a reason to consider your community.
- You are giving your businesses their best opportunity to attract customers and make sales.
- You are giving your existing citizens a place where they can show pride and enthusiasm for where they live.
- You are displaying to the outside world that your city is strong in their management of local ordinances and rules.
- You are showing that in this community, high standards are encouraged and expected.

When I am asked to perform a windshield tour, if I am familiar with the community and have friends or clients who live there, I will arrange for an associate to conduct the tour instead. I firmly believe these tours should be done with fresh eyes and no preconceived notions. If I've already been to the community, I've already had my first impression experiences—and they probably weren't documented.

To maintain objectivity, I coordinate with other trusted consultants. We exchange tours—I do one for them, and they do one for me. Occasionally, I'll have more than one person conduct a tour, allowing us to gain multiple perspectives.

Once several tours are completed by different sets of eyes, the most pressing priorities will naturally rise to the top. I've been using this approach for years with solid results.

These are the general categories that are included in my **Windshield Tour Template:**

1. City Ingress & Egress
2. City Infrastructure
3. City Services
4. Community Identity
5. Retail Area/Commercial Area

6. Downtown
7. Educational Facilities
8. Cultural/Social Impression
9. Medical Facilities
10. Industrial Parks and Areas
11. Community Services
12. Parks & Recreation
13. Housing & Neighborhoods
14. Things That Stand Out

Under each of these categories are ten areas that are judged with an assessment rating. They could include the following criteria (among any others you want to add):

- Identifiability
- Visibility
- Appearance
- Cleanliness
- Creativity
- Accessibility
- Promotions
- Convenience
- Safety
- Range of Services

Each of these criteria is then rated. You could use a five-point scale such as the following:

A sample rating key:
1. Not so good Needs serious attention.
2. Fair Could be much better.
3. Passable Could use some improvement.
4. Good In pretty good shape.
5. Excellent Well done.

As you can see, this provides a very thorough evaluation of the impression your community is making.

You don't have to hire someone to do this. Contact a friend or associate from another town and trade services. Ask them to take a drive-through, take some photos, and share with you what they see, what they liked, and what they had some issues with. Then, you do the same for them.

Again, not rocket science, but very important to the overall vitality of your community. You do not see your community the same way someone else does.

For example, you may have kids in school, so you notice when the flowers are planted, when there's trash collecting on the fences, or when the parking lot has a big pothole you have to drive around. But those who do not have kids in school might not even notice that. You may have a downtown business, so you notice when the flower barrels are damaged, when the business across the street has dirty windows, or when the building next door has a ripped canopy.

You may have a commercial business on the highway, so you notice if cars continually drive by without stopping, when a flagpole is broken and in disrepair, or when the train tracks across the highway are collecting trash. You may live out in the country and only come into town for groceries or a trip to the hardware store, so you don't notice that downtown is suffering, the murals are tired, or the junk cars on Main Street are an eyesore.

I implore the community (I actually beg them) not to take the results personally. The positive things noted in the report should be celebrated. The items that need work should be considered constructive criticism. Remember, these are practically strangers conducting the tours. They have no dog in the fight. No hidden agendas. They do not know the backstory, the excuses, or the reasons something is the way it is. They are simply telling you, "This is my impression." It is up to the community to determine how to react to the report. The whole point of the exercise is to identify points of positivity and areas that can be improved.

Now that I'm able to show a community what I see by sharing video, it does make it easier for them to see what I see. It is simply hard to really look at something you may drive by ten times a week, going to and from work, when it is not essential to your day.

You look away.

Having someone complete a visual windshield tour every few years will help keep your community looking its Sunday best. It is a highly effective program in building a foundation for aesthetic improvements. It's not a judgment of programs, services, or internal activities—it's just the visual impression a community provides to residents, visitors, and prospects.

Years ago, when I was still doing windshield tours by taking photos, I was hired to do a windshield tour, an action plan, and a marketing plan for a rural community in a Midwest state. Since I had never been to the community before, it was a perfect opportunity to start with the windshield tour. I completed the tour, taking note of the things that I identified as special and also some of the visible areas that needed some attention.

As I was going through the slideshow, the city council and EDC board seemed very engaged, often making comments about a property, offering ideas, or taking note of my suggestions. I was systematically going up and down the main business corridors in town as well as the highways. As I continued down a specific route, I noticed that the group had grown quieter and quieter. There was less banter, the comments became sparse, and then—total silence.

Along a particular route, I reached a vacant lot located on the highway, right in the middle of town. This was the intersection where one would turn toward the downtown district. It was one of the most visible corners in the community. The lot was overgrown with weeds, had trash gathered along the fence, and contained old equipment piled up in the far corner, practically covered by years of high weeds. Ironically, a beautiful "Visit Downtown" billboard stood on the highway corner of the property, inviting people to turn toward downtown.

Everyone (except me) knew what was coming. No one warned me, no one stopped me, and everyone just sat in terrified silence. I had no idea what was going on, and as I quickly flipped through the photos and videos, I reached the images of that corner. I showed the photos, complimented the beautiful sign, and made some suggestions for improvement. I casually remarked that the lot might be sending mixed messages about turning the corner to downtown, then moved on to the next property.

The mayor then stopped the meeting and asked me to go back to the previous slide that had three photos of the property taken from three different directions. I went back to that slide. He didn't say anything— just stared at the screen for what felt like 20 minutes (though it was actually about two minutes).

And then he spoke. He apologized to the city council and to the EDC board. He indicated that he never drove from that direction, he always came into town from a different highway and he never even thought about the property. It didn't have one of his businesses on it, so it was "out of sight, out of mind."

No one said anything.

Oh Good Lord of Mercy.

It was the mayor's property.

I had no idea. I didn't mean to embarrass him, but he was clearly embarrassed. I could tell he was upset. I felt terrible, and my heart was breaking for him. I didn't know what to do. So I thanked him for his comments, for all he had done for the community over the years, and for that beautiful *"Visit Downtown"* sign. I reassured him that everything else was easily fixed, then moved on to the next property and quickly wrapped up the slides and the report.

Of course, he waited for me after the meeting. I suspected my contract would be canceled and that my time in that community was over. I tried to apologize, but he said, "For what? For doing your job?"

He thanked me for my professionalism and asked me to provide him with some ideas on how that property could be best used for the community. At the next meeting, I brought him five different ideas. He reviewed them, liked one, made some tweaks, and turned it into something special—a small pocket park and dog park where travelers can stop and let their dogs play. Visitors can park, walk down Main Street, grab an ice cream or a snow cone, and enjoy a break from their drive while their dogs burn off some energy.

A brick wall on the far side of the property now displays professionally designed logos of downtown businesses for promotion. The garden club placed barrels of seasonal flowers under the "Visit Downtown" sign. The mayor had additional lights installed to keep the area well-lit at night for safety and to discourage loitering.

It became a gathering place. Local residents started grabbing lunch and meeting friends there for a quick picnic. Nearby employees would take a break, grab a book, and read in the park. What was once an eyesore became a shining star in the community. All the mayor had to do was clean it up, lay some asphalt for a small parking lot, add benches, picnic tables, water, lighting, and fencing for the dog park. Twice a month, the employees of his private business—not the city—meet there early for breakfast tacos. They mow, pick up trash, clean up the dog park, and keep everything in order.

It was painful to get to this point—for everyone involved. But all's well that ends well.

No one in that community was ever going to say anything to the mayor about his property. They liked and respected him too much. But it was an eyesore, and it didn't reflect the vibrant, dynamic downtown they had worked so hard to create. And he didn't even realize it. He was gracious. And I was relieved.

That whole episode taught me a lot about grace. He asked for grace from the community to make it right, and they gave it to him. And he extended grace to me for unwittingly putting him in an embarrassing situation. For that, I'm eternally grateful.

Look at your community with fresh eyes.

Most of the issues are easily fixed. You can grab my bonus **Windshield Tour Template** by clicking the QR Code at the back of this book.

Don't be defensive.

Don't take it personally.

Just accept it as helpful information and take action.

Most of all, don't look back. Just look forward. If you care enough to have a windshield tour done, then you care about your community. You might not like all of the results, but you care. And that is the most important ingredient in putting together positive action for improvements.

People who don't care don't ask for help.

You obviously care.

WORK *the plan*

YES, IT IS POSSIBLE to experience organic growth. Organic growth occurs without any effort from the community. It may happen due to geographic location, natural resources, proximity to industry expansion, global market needs, or other external factors. However, organic growth is not sustainable—it is out of your control.

When a piece of property is sold and a prospect purchases it to create jobs, it is considered growth. But was that the highest and best use of that property? Could that new business have been clustered with others to maximize profits? Is your available property zoned properly? Does your residential and commercial growth feel haphazard? Are you marketing your city to prospects that would bring the kind of salaries that enhance the community's quality of life? How will they impact housing, schools, and social services?

Every city needs a vision. Every county needs a vision. Every economic development corporation needs a vision. Every chamber, hospital district, and school ISD needs a vision. In the most successful cities, these entities work together to ensure that their visions, plans, hopes, and dreams complement each other with the same growth goals.

At best, they align with one another, and each entity supports objectives related to economic growth. After all, if the EDC is recruiting or expanding an existing industry that creates 100 jobs, key questions must be considered. Where will those employees live? Will they have children in the schools? Can the hospital accommodate the growth? Can city and county roads handle additional truck traffic? Are there jobs available for trailing spouses or partners? Can local businesses provide the necessary construction materials and labor? Are there even 100 people available with the appropriate skill set to fill those jobs?

At the very least, these entities must ensure that their efforts are not conflicting or redundant.

All things to consider…

When planning for economic development, the goal is to create and maintain a strong, vibrant local economy. Local economic development planning is part of a region's overall economic development strategy and requires intergovernmental coordination. The economic development plan provides a comprehensive overview of the economy, sets policy direction for growth, and identifies strategies, programs, resources, and projects to improve economic conditions.

These are the top six reasons why a strong economic development vision plays a critical role in any region's economy:

1. Job creation
2. Business diversification
3. Business retention and expansion
4. Economic fortification
5. Increase in tax revenue
6. Improved quality of life for your residents

Lesson Learned: You wouldn't build a house or take off for a cross-country vacation without a blueprint or map, so why would you leave the future of your community at risk with no plan? When I first drive into a city, I can tell immediately if they are flying by the seat of their pants or operating under some semblance of a plan. A blueprint for economic growth will help you achieve directional and intentional growth, resulting in the quality of life you desire. Organic growth is good, but controlling, pursuing, funding, and marketing for an economy that enhances your community's vision is even better. It's critical for sustainability.

My disclaimer: I'm a huge proponent of action plans, not strategic plans. It is my experience that a short-term action plan of three to five years is the most effective and successfully implemented approach. Short, concise, bold, plausible, ambitious, and measurable action—filled with quick wins, mid-term tangible projects, and priorities—will lay the foundation for bigger things. I don't include any priorities or action items without details on how to do it, the expected time frame and cost, the needed partners, the potential resources, and the anticipated outcome. This is how you get people to buy into the dream: invite them along and show them the blueprint on how to get there.

Don't depend on organic growth. You can appreciate it and celebrate it, but don't depend on it. Take your destiny into your own hands. You don't need an elaborate, expensive strategic plan that takes months and months to develop. You know what needs to be done. Gather the changemakers and stakeholders, outline it, write it up, and get going. Then, once you've done so, remind the community again and again what they said their priorities were.

You also don't have to hire an expensive consultant to do this for you. No one knows your community like your stakeholders do. It's not necessary to hire me or any other "expert" if it's not needed or not in your budget. Many communities have experienced local facilitators who can organize the discussion and keep it moving.

Sometimes, it's helpful to have an outside perspective—someone who can help you see what you might be too close to. There are several great facilitators and planners who can do an excellent job for your community and help kick-start a path of activity and growth initiatives. An outside consultant can provide perspective, experience, case studies, organization, and inspiration. But your community also has the power to get started without the expense or time of outside assistance. It just takes local commitment, a desire for results, accountability, respect for all voices, and a strong common vision to get off high center and start moving forward.

My favorite action plans have been drawn on a napkin or on the back of a conference program over a lunch or bar discussion.

Example: I once did an action plan that had eight major priorities. The community did a great job of really putting in the time and effort to evaluate and come up with their priorities. So I had refrigerator magnets made with those eight points listed on it. I delivered over 200 magnets to the community and asked them to put them on their fridges, filing cabinets, cash registers, etc. This way, no matter where they went, they were reminded of the priorities they said they wanted. But the community took it one step further.

When a priority was completed, they started marking them out or checking them off. It was a reminder of their progress and motivation. At the end of three years, when their plan was complete and their priorities had been achieved, they discussed how the visual reminder was great to keep them on task. When we did their next action plan, of course, the magnets were part of the process. If your priorities can be sufficiently bold, precise, and concise and can be put on a refrigerator magnet, then they are achievable.

Some of my best and boldest, most audacious ideas have happened in the car and spoken into my phone recorder. My most recent action plan was developed on a two-hour flight and typed out on my cell phone notes page: *Priorities, Action, Timeline, Costs, Expected Outcome,* and *Measurability*.

Click. Sent. Done.

It's not brain surgery. To repeat: don't get hung up thinking you need a big, expensive strategic plan. You don't. You just need some priorities, some actions to achieve them, and some enthusiastic stakeholders.

Action creates hope. Hope creates enthusiasm. Enthusiasm is contagious. Excitement is a magnet. Just start.

You can do it.

Just. Start. Now.

YOU NEED
good bones

IN ECONOMIC DEVELOPMENT, we consider infrastructure the "bones" of your community. Do you have good, strong bones? Or are they weak, fractured, or at risk?

When considering the health of your infrastructure, we are talking about many different facets. A community checklist of infrastructure includes water, sewage, roads, bridges, drainage, curbs and gutters, ADA accessibility, sidewalks, drainage, electric, gas, telecommunications, internet, broadband, Wi-Fi access, rail, airport/airstrips, and more.

And just like the bones in our body, all types of infrastructure should have periodic and in-depth assessments. The maintenance of infrastructure is an ongoing responsibility and should be consistently budgeted for to prevent gradual deterioration.

Our cities are now 100 to 250 years old. Roads, water lines, utilities, curbs and gutters, sewage systems, and other essential infrastructure must be maintained, replaced, and renewed to provide a modern quality of life for residents and future prospects. Numerous funding programs are available to assist with infrastructure maintenance and replacement, but they often involve a complex application process, making them difficult to access in emergency situations.

Staying informed and up to date on these programs will greatly benefit the city, county, schools, hospitals, and all entities involved in the installation and upkeep of critical infrastructure. Everything wears out eventually, and new technologies, equipment, and materials make it easier to provide a strong foundation for your community's economy.

When economic development efforts operate at a highly effective level, the taxes generated from consistent sales tax, ad valorem tax, and fees become valuable investments for the community when used efficiently for infrastructure installation and maintenance. After all, your citizens deserve safe, clean, strong, and reliable infrastructure.

Lesson Learned: It might already be a part of your city's annual planning, but if not, stop and take an inventory and assessment of the condition, date installed, and expected date or repair or replacement of *all* of your local infrastructure. It is critical for the health of your community to be aware of the condition of your bones, and to make a strong multi-year plan for replacement, repairs, and new installations. It is much more "budget effective" to do regular assessments of your infrastructure than to deal with an emergency. You will want to be proactive in making sure all your infrastructure bones remain strong, resilient, and in great working condition. Just as we do what we can to keep our own bones healthy, so we should do the same with our community's infrastructure.

LOVING THE BUSINESSES
you already have

ENGAGING AND ASSISTING BUSINESSES to stay and grow in your community should remain the primary function of economic development efforts and their closest partners. Business retention is a well-recognized best practice that consistently provides a high return on investment for economic development organizations.

Effective retention and expansion efforts require building face-to-face relationships and providing superior customer service to existing businesses. These efforts should be complemented by well-designed incentives, business-friendly services, and thoughtful coordination with local, regional, and state partners.

Structure your BRE initiatives to serve several purposes. As you meet with individual companies in your community, here are some action items to consider:

- Educate the company about the EDC, City, and other local services.
- Collect answers to both a standard series of questions *and* customized questions to quantify issues the company is facing, and determine trends and common challenges within the overall business base.
- Identify opportunities to aid local businesses that are facing challenges, thereby retaining those companies in the City/ETJ/County.

- Inquire as to staffing and skills needed to operate at full capacity.
- Identify companies that are expanding operations within and outside your market or commuting territory.
- Probe supplier attraction opportunities that would benefit existing companies.
- Identify companies considering relocating outside of the community.
- Capture testimonies from local companies about why they have chosen your community as their business location.
- Facilitate introductions and/or provide information that is requested or deemed helpful.

In my earliest days of economic development, I was tasked with creating new primary jobs. We believed that was the core role of an economic developer, and we all agreed that's what I should focus on. So, I worked hard to reach out to agriculture-based companies that would be a good fit for the assets in our small community.

Through my outreach, I connected with a company looking for a site to serve as a supply chain provider for the pork industry. We were smack dab in the middle of cattle country, but it wasn't a stretch. There were pork production facilities north and east of us in surrounding states, and the company recognized our strategic location. We were already 20 miles north of a large beef packing plant, so while no packing plants were permitted, a mid-level supply chain company was an easy fit. We were located on two major highways, meaning the additional truck traffic could be absorbed. The company didn't require incentives—only assistance with a small tax abatement to help during the early construction phase. They made multiple visits, met with the appropriate leadership, and toured several sites. Ultimately, they selected a site, put down an option, and prepared their announcement.

It just so happened that my first annual meeting of the economic development organization was taking place that month, and I asked if they would like to join us. I didn't put them on the program; I simply wanted them to meet more community stakeholders and feel appreciated for choosing us for their expansion.

Only… some crazy things happened on the way to the banquet. More than three decades later, the following events remain seared into my memory.

The company representatives stood up at the end of the banquet program and asked if they could say a few words. They came to the podium, told the community how thrilled they were to become a partner in the future of our small town, and praised the work of the EDC, the City, and the County. They complimented the farmers and agriculture-based businesses. They gave a shout-out to the school and expressed how excited their employees would be to live there. It was a magical night, and I was in economic development heaven. Their company press release went out the next day, along with photos from the banquet.

And then, two things happened to a rookie economic developer.

First, I learned the hard way that an announcement is only that.

An announcement.

I very naively thought we had the project firmly in hand. Little did I know that once the announcement went public, surrounding cities — who had no idea this company was even considering the region — came in blazing with offers of free land, big incentives, and promises out the wazoo. Within a month, the company came back and apologetically informed us they were locating 45 miles away in a different state. They paid their option, said no harm, no foul, thanked us for our time, and walked away.

We were devastated. I vowed right then and there that I would never trust an announcement until the building was built, payroll was met, and the product was rolling off the line. I learned that no project is a done deal until much, much later in the process, that an announcement is still in the beginning, squishy stage — not the end. I can't begin to tell you how many groundbreakings and announcement events I've attended since that time that never ultimately resulted in the promised outcome.

I'm pretty good now at predicting which ones will never create a single job.

It's a very sad skill to have.

Secondly, I share this story to make a wider point. The entire time I was working to woo that company — rolling out the red carpet, wining and dining, extolling all the virtues of our community — our local grocery store was struggling. Just about the time I was notified that the company wasn't coming after all, I was also told there was a good chance we were going to lose our grocery store.

Our grocery store. The one that had been there for decades. A major employer. A major taxpayer. A major supporter of youth and civic organizations. Its owners had served on the city council and school board. They had been Little League coaches, supporters of the country club, and donors to the Meals on Wheels program and senior center.

They were struggling, and we didn't even notice. We didn't even ask. I hadn't even met with them yet. I was so focused on landing the big project that I failed to see we were about to lose the one thing our community absolutely could not afford to lose. We were at least 30 miles from the nearest grocery store, and ours was a grocery hub for many small farming communities around us. People weren't as mobile then as they are now. That store was one of the critical pillars of our community.

To put this in perspective, what good would it have done to create 40 new jobs coming in the front door if we were about to lose 50 jobs and a long-time employer out the back door? It wouldn't have just been a net loss in jobs—we would have lost long-time residents, kids in schools, community volunteers, and precious neighbors.

We quickly, with all hands on deck, worked with the grocery store owners and management to get them back on solid footing, but the realization was a punch in the face.

No one loves recruiting or launching a new business more than me. The excitement of creating shiny new jobs and capital investment is the frosting on the economic development cake. But there is no cake without an existing healthy business base. They are the foundation of the community.

This was a stark lesson for me. I'm all for doing outside marketing and implementing recruitment strategies, but never "in place of" local business retention and expansion initiatives. And I can assure you that I have never taken prospects on any community visit, in the past three decades, when they didn't get back in the van and talk about "how" the community treated their existing businesses.

They notice. So should you.

As one of our favorite Texas bands, Asleep at the Wheel, would say…

"You got to dance with the one who brung you
Swing with the one who swung you
Life ain't no forty-yard dash
Be in it for the long run
In the long run, you'll have more fun
If you dance with the one who brung you
Swing with the one who swung you
Dance with the one who brung you to the bash."

We are smart people. We can multi-task like maniacs. But if I had to choose one leg of the economic development stool for you to focus on first (BRE, Recruitment, Entrepreneurship), I'd say go with your existing businesses first. A viable, healthy, thriving existing business base will be a magnet and inspiration for the other two legs.

And thank your local grocery store. It's the hardest business to sustain in Rural America. They need extra hugs. ☺

THE RURAL
resurgence

IT'S AN EXCITING TIME to be in Rural America.

In early 2018, my internal research data showed me that there was a very slight uptick in the number of people moving *from* the metro areas into rural areas. This was an interesting data point that caught my attention. In the few years leading up to that moment, I had noticed the numbers tightening: we weren't seeing the large exodus of people leaving rural communities for the cities as we had in the three decades prior. In fact, I believed that if we could just stabilize those numbers into more of an "even-steven" scenario, that would be a win for Rural America.

For decades, we watched helplessly as our youth left after high school graduation, moving to larger cities for jobs, higher education, and a different quality of life. No judgment there—I loved my hometown, but still couldn't wait to leave and experience what the big, exciting world had to offer.

Small cities that weren't actively recruiting or developing new businesses and residents experienced a slow drip, drip, drip of population loss. We bemoaned the situation and asked, "How do we keep our kids here?" The truth is, many of our youth loved where they grew up and would have stayed if they had been able to build a life there—if there had been stable employment with living wages, affordable housing, and excellent education for their young families. But if there weren't jobs, how could they stay?

At the same time, I began noticing several trends happening simultaneously, leading to a small but positive shift back to Rural America.

And this shift, I should note, was already happening before the pandemic forced us all to change our way of thinking.

1. Rural communities, with a much broader audience, were doing a better job of selling themselves to new and expanding companies.
2. The expanded ability to transfer goods from production to the market was allowing rural communities to promote their geographic locations and lower cost of doing business as a draw for solid primary job growth.
3. Promoting trade education in high schools and community colleges gave young people the ability to learn a much-needed trade and be in great demand for their skill sets.
4. Advances in technology and connectivity allowed a new generation of employees to work remotely and not have to choose between career and quality of life, in terms of choice of residence. They could enjoy both.
5. The introduction of "mega-sites" needed for large expansion projects allowed many small cities to put together acreage for large projects that could only be done in the rural regions of the country. A strong belief in regionalism, aggressive economic development organizations, visionary utility companies, and supportive landowners were the key to propelling rural economic development opportunities to a whole new level.

These tenants, and others, seem to be pulling the pendulum back towards Rural America in a way that we have not seen in decades.

It was for this reason, among others, that I created the Stand Up Rural America Summit. After starting my economic development consulting firm in 2018, I immediately began planning an event that would help rural communities across the U.S. be ready for the opportunities coming their way. Perceptions were changing, companies were becoming more open-minded about location decisions, and people were experiencing more freedom to live where they wanted. It was an exciting time to be from Rural America.

My dream was to bring together rural changemakers and trailblazers from across the country—to help educate others on how to get ready, stay ready, use technology, tell their stories, promote their assets, and grow their communities from within. I also wanted this event to provide candid lessons learned, encourage preparedness, and help communities build strong foundations to better sustain the ups and downs of economic cycles.

Most of all, I wanted to celebrate everything that makes Rural America great—the people, the history, the rich heritage, the pride, and the incredible innovators and companies that have shaped the rural communities we enjoy today.

And I wanted to share my research that was telling me: "Get ready, Rural America: your time is coming."

And guess what? That time came.

By 2019, the intensity of the spotlight on Rural America was growing, and so were the opportunities for our communities to thrive. We rolled out our first Stand Up Rural America Summit.

And then came March of 2020—the month that will live in infamy. The "stay home for a few weeks until we figure this pandemic thing out" turned into two years of disruption, chaos, isolation, and fear.

We were already poised to be in a strong position to attract business and commerce before the pandemic, but then that crisis added even more reasons to the list of "Why Rural?":

1. People sought to avoid population density. Those who had the ability to move out of cities did so. Many initially intended to leave only temporarily, but a high percentage fell in love with rural life and stayed.
2. Safety became a more pressing concern. As unrest spread across the U.S., many sought a quieter, more stable, and calmer environment outside of urban areas.
3. Technology opened new possibilities. It allowed us to promote small cities as places where people could work remotely, enjoy the outdoors, build relationships with neighbors, and pursue economic prosperity for their families.

Suddenly, people wanted a little acreage. They bought baby goats and chickens. They worked from home. Their children attended online school. They breathed clean air. They avoided the hour-long commutes to the office.

Time does not stand still, and we will once again have to adjust to a rapidly changing global market. But the spotlight was put on Rural America—and we embraced it. Rural America is now experiencing opportunities like never before.

So I ask you: Are you ready?

BUILDING A HOTBED
of entrepreneurism

SMALL BUSINESSES PLAY A CRITICAL ROLE in your business landscape. They provide key goods and services to the city's firms, residents, and workforce. Small businesses also create a ladder of opportunity for many segments of the population.

Additionally, emphasis should be placed on fostering small businesses that enhance the city and county's competitiveness by providing goods and services most desired by businesses, workers, and residents. This initiative should focus on ensuring that business development services reach all segments of the community and support the community's identified small business needs.

However, a word of caution: not every small business is a good fit for your community's population. Just because you love children's clothing doesn't mean a children's boutique can be supported by the local market. Likewise, you may want to open a day spa, but be sure there is a strong potential customer base to sustain it. People will drive to a neighboring city for certain products or experiences, but your marketing strategy must reflect that reality.

I love small businesses and want every one of them to be successful. However, in a rural community, it's essential to ensure that the numbers work. A solid business plan—one that clearly outlines the number of customers or revenue needed for sustainability—is critical to success.

Action Items to Consider:

- Support access to high-speed internet throughout the community.
- Maintain a database of available commercial and retail properties.
- Promote entrepreneurship by serving as a "connector" between local entrepreneurs and the necessary resources they seek (e.g., talent, capital, networks).
- Encourage local school districts and other local K-12 educational institutions to incorporate entrepreneurship courses into their academic curricula.
- Link small business growth to the city's and county's existing large corporations.
- Create a central database for RFPs from your large corporations seeking subcontracting or vendor services. Make the database available to all companies in your community, providing opportunities for young and emerging companies.
- Small businesses could become "prequalified" to serve as a vendor to large corporations.
- Create an "Innovation District" in your community. This will attract technology-related industries such as Skills Development Training, Research and Development, Start-Ups, Business Services, Entrepreneurial Support, and more.
- Prioritize public policies (e.g., zoning and land use regulations) and infrastructure investments that make the commercial district more attractive to entrepreneurs and start-ups.
- Designate a special "fiberhood" in a commercial or downtown district, with access to ultra-high-speed internet to attract technology start-ups and entrepreneurs. Create marketing efforts that target specific types of businesses to expand and relocate into this district. An example would be technology providers, graphic designers, digital marketing agencies, remote medical services, skills training, etc.
- Identify and assist in the outreach and recruitment of specific businesses to reduce retail leakage.
- Promote your city as the perfect place for remote workers.
- Sponsor an Information Packet for interested small business owners and entrepreneurs. Provide readily available information for discussions, including business plan resources, available sites

and buildings, market data, funding sources, agency assistance, and more. Include details on your designated Small Business Development Center (SBDC), Small Business Administration (SBA) office, and other small business resources.

- Sponsor workshops and programs led by the SBA, SBDCs, and local professionals on key topics such as business planning, taxes, legal issues, workforce development, marketing, and administration. If these activities are already taking place, be proactive in promoting and supporting them within the community. If they aren't, consider sponsoring a series of Lunch-N-Learns or Beers with Peers Educational Programs to engage business owners.

- Establish a Revolving Loan Fund specifically for small or downtown businesses. Apply for funding through the USDA and EDA, which offer one-time-use funds for these types of projects. Work with the city or county to serve as the sponsoring host, establish loan criteria, and create an application process.

- Sponsor a Façade and Signage Matching Grant Program. The appearance of local business districts is a critical factor in their success. First impressions of a community can directly impact business viability and sustainability. There are multiple ways to establish and administer these programs.

- Likewise, sponsor an Interiors and Equipment Matching Grant Program. While exterior aesthetics are important, the inside of a business matters just as much. What a disappointment it would be for a beautifully renovated exterior to house an interior in need of repairs, updated furniture, or necessary fixtures to function as a viable business. This is another reason to establish a Revolving Loan Fund or provide access to capital on a matching basis.

- Sponsor a "Big Idea" contest for students and adults. This is a great way to foster entrepreneurial spirit. These contests have been successful in every community where they have been implemented. Consider establishing clear criteria, valuable prizes, and widespread promotion to maximize participation.

- Support or sponsor co-working, shared space, or incubator space for small businesses in their infancy. Sometimes, entrepreneurs and remote workers simply need to be around others, work outside of their homes, or share expenses. New workers, remote employees, traveling professionals, and start-ups can all benefit from access to co-working or incubator space.

- Utilize social media to aggressively promote local businesses. Create and promote a hashtag for businesses to use, increasing visibility and social shares. Consider hiring a summer intern to create content for each business, scheduling posts in advance for ongoing promotion. Encourage a "shop local" mindset and foster partnerships between businesses for special events, sales, customer appreciation days, and regional outreach efforts.

NOTE: The Bonus Resources at the end of this book provide samples of successful examples of these Action Items.

A common fear—and a valid one—is that mom-and-pop stores will struggle to compete with Walmarts, Dollar Generals, and national tire and oil change shops that set up in or near your community. Short of owning all available private property in the city or enforcing rigid zoning ordinances, it's difficult to keep a national chain out of the community.

These businesses often do not ask for incentives: their market research tells them where to locate, and they find a site owned by someone willing to sell. This can be tough on the existing business base, so I'm not making light of it at all. But it is a reality, and I don't see the trend reversing.

So, you have two options: give up (which is a horrible choice), or tweak your business to take advantage of the circumstances. If a new Walmart is opening on the edge of town and attracting people from neighboring communities, look at it as a whole new pool of potential customers.

Admittedly, it's hard to compete with the price or volume of discount stores. But it's not at all hard to showcase exceptional customer service. Instead of going head-to-head with them, differentiate yourself. If you sell school supplies, advertise that for every bundle purchased from your store, a donation will be made to local and nearby schools. If you sell tires, offer free rotations for two years with a tire purchase. If you run a home goods store, provide a coupon on each holiday for a discount on the next holiday.

For example, give a Christmas coupon that's valid for Valentine's Day, then a Valentine's coupon for Easter, and so on. This builds a pipeline of returning customers throughout the year. Use your imagination—give visiting shoppers a reason to stop by your business as well.

When competing with Walmart, Dollar General, or a fast-food franchise, you can't just complain about it or try to shame your community into avoiding them. That is a futile strategy. You need to give people a reason to shop with you—good products, clean facilities, welcoming staff, reliable hours, superior customer service, delivery options, and customer appreciation initiatives. While the community may not have wanted large discount stores to locate nearby, these businesses will enhance the tax base, create a variety of jobs, and often provide a new reason for consumers to visit the community.

You can do it. Whether you have a big discount store nearby or not… be who you are, offer a great business, and be a big supporter of the community. That will allow you to stand out.

For all of the right reasons.

BRINGING NEW LIFE
to old bricks

EVERYONE DESERVES ACCESS to a vibrant neighborhood—a place with a thriving local economy, rich character, and inviting public spaces that make residents and visitors feel welcome. Yet, we know that many Americans, whether in small towns or big cities, miss out on these benefits.

The need for downtown revitalization initiatives grew from the recognition that a community is only as strong as its core. In an era when many had given up hope on the commercial and cultural viability of downtown, and when suburbs, shopping malls, and big-box retailers dominated the American landscape, revitalization seemed like an unlikely proposition. But over the last four decades, time has proven that downtowns are the heart of our communities. And we need a healthy heart—not one on life support.

Communities set their own destinies. It is not someone else's job to come in and save your downtown. While revitalization is challenging (and expensive) work, many models and case studies offer a road map for locally owned, locally driven prosperity. Across the country, thousands of communities have transformed their downtowns, resulting in expanded economies, increased social interaction, vibrant gathering spaces, dynamic entrepreneurship, increased tourism dollars, needed green space, expanded activities, leveraged local leadership, and an overall improved quality of life.

Understandably, people often resist change. But change is inevitable.

Technology, the economy, demographics, population growth, market trends, and consumer attitudes are constantly evolving—and they will affect a community whether people like it or not. There are only two kinds of change in the world today: planned change and unplanned change. You can plan for a vibrant downtown, or you can leave it to chance. And we all know what can happen when the future is left to chance.

You can't avoid the hard conversations forever. I'm 99% certain that your community has building owners with substandard properties—owners who overestimate their property's value, absentee owners, and even belligerent owners. From my experience working with multiple cities, I have found that a soft conversation about their needs, their plans, and their legacy is far more effective than a tough conversation about how bad their property looks or how much of an eyesore it is to the community. That approach will get you nowhere. Through hundreds of conversations with downtown building owners, I've found the following scenarios to be common:

- They are hanging on to it because it might be one of the last assets they have.
- They are not interested in selling because they are using it for storage (this is the easiest one to provide a solution for).
- They know it's dilapidated, but do not have the resources to fix it up into a market-ready or sellable condition.
- In their minds it is worth what they "need" it to be worth to fit into their retirement needs, not what the market or condition says it's worth.
- They are simply overwhelmed and embarrassed and willing to do something, but don't know how or where to start.
- They are suspicious that offers for purchase are all from a point of "taking advantage of them."
- Finally, they are sentimentally attached and are worried that if the building changes owners or uses, the community will forget about them and their contributions to the economic prosperity of the community in former years. Their fear of being forgotten is paralyzing to them.

To assist in the development of a blueprint for downtown revitalization, I urge you to implement the following:

- **Capture** the vision of your revitalized downtown.
- **Develop** a serious and aggressive short-action plan that includes responsibility, accountability, and measurability.
- **Assign** the task of speaking to building owners to someone who has a positive outlook and without a financial interest in the outcome.
- **Forge** healthy private/public partnerships.
- **Assess** the condition of buildings, infrastructure, lighting, parking, accessibility, utilities, traffic flow, etc.
- **Establish** business improvement districts and other non-profits dedicated to downtown improvements.
- **Identify** the organization responsible for implementation.
- **Identify** an entertainment/hospitality district, as their needs may be different than traditional retail.
- **Develop** policies for second-story living, residential rentals, and food/vendor/retail trucks and pop-ups.
- **Develop** a local-serving retail strategy and entrepreneurship support programs.
- In addition to business development, clean-up/demo days, safety issues, aesthetics, etc., should also be considered.
- **Ensure** every segment of your population is involved in the revitalization activities.
- **Tell** the world everything you are doing. Every improvement project. Every activity. Every partner. Every business. Every contributor. Every result.

Tell. The. World.

Observations: Three things…

1. Don't wait for permission. Grab a friend and start making little improvements. It will jumpstart the desire to create space that is welcoming to the community. Pick up trash. Sweep the sidewalk. Plant flowers. Add a bench. Paint a sign. Wash the windows. Hold an outdoor yoga class. Hold a book club meeting on the square.

2. Don't get hung up on things like parking. No amount of parking spaces will enhance the taste of the coffee someone is buying or the food the café is serving. I promise you: if you have a vibrant business, people will figure out how to get there. Start with the empty buildings, the clean-up, the sidewalks, and lighting enhancements. Then, promote the existing businesses and the opportunities for new businesses. Hold downtown events. Promote the area as a gathering place. Do all you can to make it pedestrian-friendly.

3. Don't assume that the City's hands are tied. They are not. The City can design and enforce ordinances that are intended to create a safe, viable downtown district. They can create rules and ordinances for building safety, aesthetics, and viability. I find that many city officials hide behind the mantra "it's their private property" as a way of avoiding the hard conversations. But you *can*, and you *should* create a set of ordinances that will create a safe, beautiful, vibrant gathering space for your citizens. No one wants to invest and revitalize a building if the one next door is a fire hazard. No one wants to invest and revitalize a building on a block that has no incentive to reach a minimum standard of acceptability by the community. And no one wants to spend time in a downtown if there are buildings that are ugly, dirty, and basically a safety hazard. We all want more than this. We yearn for this. So, get out front and incentivize the community to support efforts to create a vibrant downtown space. It will be hard, it can get ugly, and—in most cases—it will be expensive. But you need a set of expectations that aligns with the community's vision.

Set some high standards and embrace them. Develop some tough ordinances and then enforce them. Invite potential entrepreneurs to walking tours and open houses. Celebrate your businesses who are doing their best to wave the downtown banner. Hold events and say, "This is just the beginning," so that people know great things are on the horizon.

And then back it up.

Downtowns matter. Your downtown is the heart and soul of any community. You can create jobs without a healthy downtown, but you can't sustain a long-term, vibrant community without one.

Quit waiting for someone else to do the hard stuff. It's your community. Take a stand.

CREATE
gathering space

PEOPLE ARE LIKE BIRDS OF A FEATHER: we like being together. We gravitate to each other. And we love beautiful spaces. Safe spaces. We gravitate to those too.

But what do we do if there is nowhere to go?

The residents of a community need to feel connected. The best way to cultivate that connection is through shared experiences, conversations, debates, laughter, and support.

We find that there are many gathering spaces within a community where groups convene for specific reasons. Two of the most popular gathering spots in a community are for school activities or church activities. But what if our lifestyle doesn't fit into either of these spaces? How do we connect with others in our community that don't have school-aged children? Or with those of a different religious affiliation — or no religious affiliation at all?

For more than a century, that place has generally been the downtown area. People would come into town on the weekends and shop, eat, do business, and gather with their friends and neighbors. When our downtowns began to age or decline, we began to lose that connection to our neighbors. People began to travel to other neighboring cities to get their supplies. The kids went to larger communities to the multi-screen movie theaters. People were leaving instead of coming. We lost the common tie to our community.

I love it when the downtowns are revitalized back into the vibrant heartbeat of our communities. And I think every city should make that a priority, not just for the businesses and commerce, but to give your citizens that common place to gather. It could be a coffee shop, a town square, a pocket park, or benches by the post office. That place where you know you are going to run into neighbors and strangers about to become your neighbors.

Even better, create reasons to gather: farmers markets, veterans programs, kids programs, 5k races, picnics, announcements, Shakespeare in the Park, pep rallies, Santa and Easter Bunny photos, scavenger hunts… you get it—reasons to gather.

It doesn't have to be downtown. It can be anywhere in the community. A place where people gravitate. A place where people can feel togetherness, common passion for the community, and where they can experience daily life together.

The most vibrant communities will have safe and beautiful gathering spaces.

Points to Ponder: Right off the top of your head: do you have a local gathering spot? Is it a local coffee shop? The county barn? The gym? The senior center? The city park? If you say you don't know if you have a gathering space, then your residents are scattered. It's a challenge to create cohesiveness, collaboration, engagement, and pride in a community if everyone is doing their own thing.

If you know of your gathering space right away, or even have more than one in town, then you have a competitive advantage. Make it a priority to always maintain them, keep them safe, and work to keep them beautiful. It might feel like an intangible priority, but a community that knows and connects to its neighbors is a gift that will strengthen the city, in both times of need and times of prosperity. One thing that we all learned during the pandemic: we are not meant to be isolated and alone.

Give people space to gather. Give them a reason to come together. Celebrate your community and your neighbors all you can. Heck, we all have a reason to just celebrate life.

Magical things happen when people gather for positive reasons.

SHARING
spaces

I'D LIKE TO ASK YOU TO think outside of the box for a minute. Our rural communities have several challenges when promoting entrepreneurship:

- The cost of launching and maintaining the business.
- Finding a site that has the amenities that business needs.
- Providing the population to support that business.

This concept started taking off in rural communities over the past decade, and I wanted to share this thought with you.

When starting a small business, it's hard to fund it, launch it, market it, create an amazing experience for your customers, and hopefully make some profit. What if you were able to take away some of the risk in that equation?

We are all trailblazers at heart. We make our own way, do everything *our* way, and assume all of the risk and glory ourselves. But the concept of sharing spaces can be an advantage for everyone involved.

Examples: Say you want to open a bakery. You have identified the perfect downtown location, but the building is dilapidated. Your bakery budget just won't cover the renovation costs. If the optimum time for the bakery to be open is from early morning to early afternoon, then your building has the capacity to accommodate another business in the evening. What if someone else wanted to open a BBQ joint? What if they either shared the cost of the renovations or just paid rent to the bakery to use the newly renovated space? It takes some imagination, but I have seen it successfully done time after time.

Both businesses require a kitchen that meets the local health codes and permits. Both prefer a downtown location. Both need functioning restrooms for their customers. Both need some sort of seating. Perhaps the bakery faces the downtown square, and the BBQ joint faces the back of the building, where an awesome covered patio serves its customers. Perhaps they share the entire restaurant, providing a secure storage area where each will store their own kitchen pots and pans, serving dishes, etc.

In situations where space is shared, the community wins. They get two businesses instead of one, a dilapidated building restored, and less risk for the two businesses involved. Obviously, strong contracts and agreements are involved, but I have seen this work.

One of my favorite examples is when a local EDC purchased a building and took on the renovations to create a test kitchen for the community. But instead of sharing the space between tenants on a morning/evening basis, they shared it on a day-by-day basis.

Two women wanted to open a Mexican food restaurant. They rented the space on Monday, Tuesday, and Thursday to build their customer base, fine-tune their menu, and figure out their long-term needs. A different tenant rented the space on Wednesdays and Fridays for an Asian food menu. Yet a third tenant used the space on Saturdays to serve their locally "famous" hamburgers. And each Sunday, the space was reserved for local non-profits to hold fundraisers.

Over time, some tenants built up their businesses enough to move into their own locations. Others never intended to run a full-time business but benefited from the opportunity to test their concept. The return on investment for this project was excellent—everyone was a winner.

One of the neighboring communities saw the success of this project and borrowed the concept. However, instead of restaurants, they needed offices. So they purchased a small historic building and renovated it to include a few offices, a small conference room, a large conference room, a kitchen, restrooms, and a reception area.

Through their Strategic Gap Study process, they discovered that their community needed more professional services. They reached out to businesses in the nearest metro area, searching for lawyers, CPAs, graphic designers, and financial planners willing to send a representative to their community one or two days a week.

- A law firm came on Monday
- A CPA firm operated on Tuesday and Friday
- A financial planner served clients on Wednesday
- A graphic design/marketing firm took the space on Thursday

Each tenant had a private, lockable storage area for their equipment and supplies. The EDC, as the landlord, provided Wi-Fi, a printer and copy machine, a kitchen stocked with locally sourced snacks and coffee, and clear signage listing the weekly tenants. The tenants simply had to show up and serve their clients.

But wait, there's more!

This project had an unexpected bonus: it provided new customers for local businesses. The professionals often came in early or stayed overnight in local hotels. It also kept residents from traveling to a neighboring metro city for services, strengthening the local economy.

As with the test kitchen model, both the law firm and the CPA firm built up enough local clients that they eventually purchased and renovated their own office spaces and became full-time businesses in the community—freeing up the shared space for other small business services.

Job well done to both communities. By thinking outside the traditional way of doing business, they found ways to support local businesses, renovate buildings, meet residents' needs, and generate a strong return on investment. Winners all around.

I share these scenarios with you as examples of how we can do things differently, and it's okay. If your community is having the hard conversations about what assets you have, what your needs are, and what the anticipated costs will be, then you have what you need to let your imagination run wild. It was not going to be possible to get any of the tenants listed in the two examples to run with their businesses alone: it was simply not financially feasible, and they were uncertain of their customer base.

It's just the old "incubator" concept dusted off and freshened up. (We don't use that word anymore!) But if done right, it can be a tremendous asset to a community. Anything you can do to create commerce and gathering opportunities in your small city is a win.

If I started a project like this in a community, I would call it "The Hatchery." Oh, the fun we could have with that.

No one has to go it alone.

Just use one of those lawyers to create some strong tenant agreements and GO!

PAINT IS
your friend

OH, HOW I LOVE some beautiful paint. Don't get me wrong, I'm all about crisp white, bold black, steel gray, beautiful brown, Razorback Red—I love the strong traditional colors. But throw me some sage green, sky blue, perfect pink, electric orange, sunrise yellow, or passion purple, and my heart sings. Color, used in the right places, can be a beautiful addition to any community: buildings, canopies, signage, landscaping, benches—the pop of color brings a sense of vibrancy to any view.

I am a big fan of murals. I have seen an abundance of fantastic murals in my travels. They are embedded in my mind forever. Some tell a story, some depict history, and some are just simply beautiful. But some are weird, some are scary, and some just aren't very good.

I remember those, too.

When a mural is done right, it's not only a beautiful work of art, but can also improve the exterior or interior aesthetics of a building. Maybe even camouflage some of the building's flaws. They can provide directions, they can honor community members, and they can promote local industry or events.

I especially love it when a vintage mural from decades past is restored to its original brilliance. A wonderful nod to the history of the building or the community.

But the flipside of that is the collection of murals that are neglected or barely visible. A reminder of a more prosperous time. Those are the ones that pull at my heart. The ones that are barely a whisper of days gone by, but not able to celebrate the future.

I recently watched a community group fight tirelessly to prevent a new building owner from painting over an old mural on the property they had just purchased. This group protested the business to elected officials, wrote editorials accusing the owner of trying to erase history, and essentially shamed them in every way possible. I came across this situation in my research on social media, and it caught my eye. So, I delved further.

The building, located near the entrance to town, had been empty for more than two decades. It was a common two-story warehouse-style building with a brick exterior—similar to those seen in many rural communities. At one time, it had been a textile manufacturing plant, playing a dynamic role in the community's history.

But the plant had long since closed, and over the years, tenants were unable to make use of the large building, renovate it, or restore it. At one time, it had welcomed visitors to the city with a large mural painted on the exterior wall facing the highway entrance. From old photos, I could see that it was a skillful piece of work, painted in the mid-1950s when the plant was in full swing. I could also tell that, during that era, the entire downtown area was active and had an air of energy and movement.

In later photos, the mural was still visible, though it had begun to lose its vibrancy and impact. In more recent images, it was barely discernible. In fact, the faded mural likely made the building look worse than if it had never been there at all. What once served as a welcoming landmark had become a worn-out reminder of what the community used to be.

The building was more than 125 years old. The mural was around 75 years old.

I don't know about you, but at 75 years old, we can all use a little facelift or some color.

I became highly invested in the outcome of this drama.

The community activist group demanded that the new owner "not" paint over the old mural. The community activist group demanded that the new owner restore the old mural (at his expense) or else.

Or else? Or else what?

As an observer, this is what I saw.

- A person bought a building that was on private property that was legitimately for sale.
- That person bought a building that had been empty for the better part of two decades.
- That person had a right to do whatever he wanted to do with his newly purchased building as long as it was not illegal or nefarious.
- Not once in those two decades did the community activist group engage in any fundraising efforts to restore the mural.
- The community activist group never attempted to raise the funds to purchase the building and create a viable business.
- The community activist group said they were doing all of this in the name of "preserving history," but the mural had been neglected and had faded to the point where only those who had lived in the community for more than 40 years would have even known what it represented.

Through their badgering, their scathing rhetoric, and their public shaming, the new owner abandoned his plans to open his business there and moved to another city.

This was three years ago. The activist group got their way.

He did not paint over the old and faded historical mural.

He also did not create the twenty jobs he promised, restore an old but beautiful, dilapidated building, add an abandoned building back to the tax rolls, or create a new, vibrant first impression in the community.

That group has still not made any effort to raise the funds to restore the mural. So, there it sits—exactly like it did ten years ago, twenty years ago—an empty, faded reminder of how the community used to be.

That company could have been the catalyst for new growth, new business, and new residents.

Now, they will never know. All in the name of history.

My point to this story is that you can honor your history but build for the future. In their tight-fisted effort to maintain their city's history, they sacrificed new opportunities for their community.

The sad caveat to this story: The new owner was a young man who grew up in that community, went away, built up a strong manufacturing business, and wanted to bring that success back to his community. He wanted to raise his young family in the community that raised him. He was not a stranger.

We can do better.

Murals are very sentimental. When used in the right way, they are bursts of glory that are embedded in your memory forever. I have a whole workshop on how to incorporate murals into a community because the case studies are so incredible, and the ideas are endless. I have seen the most fantastic murals and works of art in our amazing rural communities.

But we should use paint for good—to enrich, to show off the talents of our students, to highlight the gifts of our local artisans, to welcome someone to a business or city, to honor the history of a trailblazer, to promote a local business or industry.

A bit of advice: I learned that not all artists are created equal. What someone can brilliantly capture on an 11" x 17" canvas does not always translate well to a 15' x 20' brick or stucco wall. Whenever possible, PLEASE use professional mural artists.

I know of incredible mural artists across the U.S. Some are gifted designers who create their own artwork, while others specialize in taking someone else's vision or artwork and successfully transferring it to an expanded space. They understand proportions, color dynamics, and the depth needed to create a vibrant, memorable mural.

I've seen murals that were created with the best intentions but fell short simply because the artist's skill set did not align with large-scale mural work. On the other hand, I've seen stunning window paintings by local artists, both young and old. There are plenty of opportunities for every level of artistic talent to be displayed in a community.

Put a fresh coat of paint on those old buildings. Freshen up your signs. Paint those dumpsters and park benches. Paint the old trim on your metal buildings.

Every building, every business, every sign has a story to tell.

It's okay if it's a new story.

Make every day a picture day.

A little paint goes a long way.

YOUR HANDY *toolbox*

IF YOU HAVE MADE IT THIS FAR into the book, then I can only believe that you truly want what's best for your community. Thank you for caring so much about the future growth and development of the city you call home.

Let's wrap up our discussion by talking about some of the tools that you have at your disposal to assist you in making good, solid, aggressive, and strategic decisions about the future of your small city.

There are many federal programs available to you as a rural community, many of them flowing through the Economic Development Administration (EDA), USDA Rural Development, Department of Veterans Affairs, Federal Office of Rural Health, Federal Housing Programs, Bureau of Indian Affairs, Department of Commerce, Administration for Children and Families, Department of Energy, Department of Health and Human Services, Department of Housing and Urban Development, Environmental Protection Agency, Federal Communications Commission, Federal Transit Administration, Internal Revenue Service, National Institutes of Health, National Park Service, Small Business Administration, and many more.

Most of our dynamic states have programming directed to their rural counties and communities. I urge you to study and learn about the programming that your state governments offer. This is the most efficient approach, especially in providing infrastructure assistance, small business assistance, workforce skills training, housing tax credits, and other non-financial types of assistance.

Work closely with your city and county governments to ensure that you are taking advantage of programs that are available to them, or work with them to create programs that will benefit your local businesses, investors, developers, and entrepreneurs. Every state that I have worked in has had some unique and successful programs. Take my advice on researching the case studies, and you will have the knowledge you need to create the perfect programs for your state or community. Also work closely with your local large utility providers, as well as your electric and telephone cooperatives. They often have innovative resources and programs specifically for rural regions. They are outstanding partners in economic growth. If you aren't working closely with them, you should be.

In addition, take the time to do a Housing Inventory Study, a Strategic Gap Study, a Traffic Study, and a Windshield Tour. These programs will be critical in your decision-making when crafting your growth initiatives moving forward.

A **Housing Inventory Study** will provide a report on the types, numbers, and condition of your existing housing inventory. Then, take that information and compare it to the types of housing needed by local industry, local schools, local government, and local medical services. In addition to analyzing the types of housing your residents want, it will take into account what they can afford. This will help in working with the appropriate housing developers and contractors to come as close as possible to meeting the needs of the community. It will also help you access housing programs that fit your specific needs. Depending on the size of your community, this can be done internally, with a summer intern, in partnership with a local community college or university, or by a professional firm that specializes in Housing Studies.

A **Strategic Gap Study** will tell you what your people are spending their money on outside of your community, such as food, groceries, home goods, pharmacy, recreation, clothing, etc. It will tell you how far consumers are willing to drive. It will tell you the retail or business gaps that your population can support. For example, perhaps you have four hair salons but no one who services men's haircuts. Perhaps your community has ten restaurants, but only two stay open past 2:00 p.m., and no one opens on Sunday or Monday. Perhaps several of your businesses indicate that they have to travel to a nearby city to obtain office supplies.

This is an opportunity for an existing business to add these products to its mix or for an entrepreneur to open an office supply store.

Perhaps you learn that more than twelve commercial businesses are contracting trucking services to move their goods from their plant to their suppliers. This is the perfect opportunity for a local entrepreneur to start a local trucking company. Perhaps none of your food providers offer organic or vegetarian options. This is an opportunity for someone to adjust their menus or for someone new to meet their needs. Perhaps you find that there is not enough childcare for ages 2–5, or there is a prevalent need for after-school tutoring.

This is the type of information a Strategic Gap Study will provide. An example from a study I conducted for one of my communities years ago: the community had eight churches, eight liquor stores, six Mexican food restaurants, and four barbecue joints. (Yes, it was a fun community!) That was it. Once we shared this with the community, they slowly began making adjustments.

After a three-year period of adjustments, the community had eight churches, four liquor stores, four bars or private clubs, three Mexican food restaurants, two burger joints, two diners/cafés, one Asian buffet, one sandwich shop, one BBQ shack, and one steakhouse. The city was located on a highway, and they marketed all their businesses together cooperatively. As a result, the profitability of all businesses increased significantly. Instead of competing with each other, their food diversity became a draw for surrounding communities, and everyone flourished. A Strategic Gap Study will highlight redundancies and opportunities. This can be conducted internally, with interns, in partnership with nearby colleges or universities, or by professionals.

A **Traffic Study** can be provided by your state or regional Department of Transportation or conducted locally. Typically, these studies are done over a set period, such as one or two weeks, to determine traffic volume, types of traffic, and peak times. These numbers are critical when approaching developers regarding potential commercial projects. They are also valuable when engaging hotels, restaurants, franchises, and companies. Additionally, traffic data is essential when working with city and county officials on safety issues, particularly at intersections, rail crossings, and over/underpasses.

For years, we tracked traffic manually by assigning people to park at designated intersections to count vehicles, identify types, and note peak times. These days, it is much easier to arrange for cameras to capture the data, which can then be analyzed in an office rather than from inside a vehicle. Again, this study can be conducted internally, with interns, in collaboration with colleges and universities, or by professionals.

Finally, I'd like to share some key options to consider for your Rural Economic Development Tool Chest. I am a strong proponent of establishing revolving loan funds and local investment groups. While most rural lenders are outstanding, they are often stretched thin and unable to fund every needed project. Our goal should be to reduce risk for all parties involved in a project.

I encourage all of my client communities to establish a Revolving Loan Fund with funding through USDA programs. I can't begin to count all of the successful projects that have resulted from utilizing local Revolving Loan Funds. These are not grants—they are loans.

By partnering with a lender and/or investor, the Revolving Loan Fund can:
- Fill a funding gap at a competitive interest rate.
- Secure loans with collateral taking a second or third lien.
- Provide initial loans for projects that may be too small for traditional lenders.

To establish a Revolving Loan Fund, all you need to do is provide matching funds to create the initial pool. From that point forward, all loan repayments are returned to the fund to be re-loaned to future projects.

Private investment plays a critical role in injecting much-needed capital into projects, businesses, or initiatives, helping bring them to successful completion. Investment groups are not intended to replace traditional lending or funding but to engage prospects, spread risk, and support the larger goals and objectives of the EDC board.

Investment Groups can be formed for one-time projects or for ongoing investments in multiple projects.

These are examples of various types of Local Investment Groups:

Own to Sell or Support with expected ROI: This type of investment group is formed to purchase property with the intention of either flipping the property for profit, supporting a new business with the ultimate goal of selling to the business, or being a limited partner or an investor in the business with an expected ROI. These investment groups operate on a limited engagement basis.

Own/Lease for Revenue: This type of investment group is formed to purchase property for lease or to invest in a business with the expectation of monthly, quarterly, or annual revenue. These are generally ongoing, long-term projects.

Own to Sell without expected ROI: This type of investment group is formed to add value to a project, get a project over the finish line, or fill a gap between market price and project completion. The underlying goal of this investment group is to provide a community service. While not expecting a loss on the projects, the overarching goal is not necessarily profit-driven.

Contributions to Specific Community Development Projects (donation): This type of investment group is formed to provide impactful contributions to the effort, including land, buildings, equipment, programming, special projects, aesthetic projects, signage, etc.

These are just a few examples of innovative tools that will help you make informed and ambitious plans for your community moving forward.

TELL YOUR STORY...

MAKE EVERYONE
an ambassador

NO ONE CAN SELL YOUR COMMUNITY like a local citizen who loves where they live and is proud to extol its virtues. But even more importantly, bringing various and diverse community organizations into the development of your identity and marketing mission will pay dividends. I'm going to refer back to the chapter where we talked about apathy—give your community something to care about. Because once people have a reason to care, that's when the magical action begins.

There are many ways to generate buy-in and enthusiasm from the community. Create a challenge for the youth to produce fun and positive TikTok videos about the community and feature them on the official EDC social media channels. Take breakfast tacos to your local manufacturing plants and capture testimonials from people who have moved into the community. Gather stories from old-timers about historical businesses or events from decades ago. Promote those stories in print, blogs, posts, and videos to show the community that you value its heritage and history. Capture quotes from local leadership about their vision for the future or goals for the year. Partner with various civic organizations to create a "you share my stuff, and I'll share yours" agreement. Chances are, at least some of your networks do not overlap, giving your message a broader reach.

Example: What if your community really wanted to reach out to dog lovers? You've created beautiful dog parks, held several dog-focused events, and featured dogs on community-wide social media channels. But why not take it a step further?

Tell the story of your community through the eyes of a dog. Attach GoPro cameras to dogs and narrate videos with different voices, depicting what the dogs might be thinking. Create videos featuring blue heelers herding cattle, poodles getting a spa day at the groomer, mutts from the local shelter visiting a nursing home, golden retrievers playing frisbee in the local parks, boxers enjoying a pup cup in the drive-through of the local coffee shop, a labrador walking their young charge to school or the bus stop, or a chihuahua in someone's purse while shopping in downtown boutiques. You get the picture. If you want to brag about being the Best Community for Dog Lovers, then believe it, show it, and live it.

Likewise, if you want to promote your affordable housing inventory, talk to residents and employees about why they love living in your community. Film the video in the neighborhoods. If they aren't comfortable on camera, get a photo and a quote or testimonial. Mix it up. If you are marketing to potential teachers, ask students what they love about their school—their favorite memories, favorite teachers, and favorite events. They will sell your school system in a human and authentic way that far surpasses anything prospective teachers could learn from school leadership.

If you love your community, your neighbors love your community and your businesses love your community, they will sell your community better than anyone else. Just be mindful to set boundaries so that it's not an avalanche of unrelated outgoing marketing. Try to keep everyone on message. And do your best to limit negativity.

Lesson Learned: Don't let individuals hijack your marketing efforts. You own your social media accounts. You are not obligated to allow citizens to say whatever they want on your pages. I love open forums if they are positive and engaging. But the minute they turn negative, then they are no longer helpful and are even detrimental to your marketing efforts. It's okay to make your posts on any social media channels "information only," meaning they are not designed to be conversations. Perhaps many of your channels will be left open for comments, but others are turned off. Don't lose control of your message or your marketing outreach by letting the naysayers take it over. Even if you get pushback, create a one-pager of all of the places where citizens can share their voice on issues: City Council Meetings, EDC Meetings, School Board Meetings, Town Hall Meetings, Social Accounts designed for dialogue, etc.

Remember that your EDC and community-focused marketing is designed for people inside the community to be reminded of your many assets and amenities and for the outside world to learn about your assets, opportunities, and history.

There are so many free or affordable tools at our fingertips now to create great content, craft dynamic messages, and tell your story to the world. Decades ago, we only had paid advertisements and traditional media avenues. There's no end to the ways you can reach your targets.

Don't be invisible. Get everyone on board. Everyone in your community can be an ambassador for you. Enthusiasm is contagious. Everyone wants to have a healthy community. Develop the plan and invite people along. No one loves a community like the people who live there. Give them a megaphone and let them tell the world why.

If you can't find those people, then that will show you that you have some work to do before inviting people and prospects over for dinner.

Find your people.

Then, give them a blazing megaphone.

YOUR *online story*

IT'S NOT A CLICHÉ to say that first impressions matter.

An economic development organization's website is its most effective marketing tool, followed by "planned visits to corporate executives" and "media relations/publicity." With nearly two-thirds (66%) of executives and location advisors indicating they are likely to visit an EDO's website during their next site search, it's more important than ever to ensure your EDO's website effectively markets and provides information about your community. Whether you're making touch-ups or considering a total site overhaul, here are some best practices to ensure your EDO website is at the top of its game.

1. **Up-To-Date Data**
    Site selectors, executives, and other decision-makers want to know if your community has the workforce needed to support their business. That's why it's important to include the most recent data sourced from a third party. For best results, make it easily accessible (within one to two clicks) from the homepage. Also, consider including supplemental information from a twenty-, forty-, and sixty-mile radius.

2. **Feature Your Key Industries**
    Location advisors, real estate managers, and potential businesses want to know what your region does best. Tout your top business sectors with a dedicated page for each industry

group. Clearly identify the sector's strategic advantages and list or provide success stories for the top employers in the region to demonstrate a robust industry network. Testimonial videos from your existing companies are the best hooks to showcase why someone should consider your community. This brings us to our next item…

3. **Showcase Leading Employers**
    Showcasing your community's leading employers is a great way to show decision-makers not only that other major companies are already thriving there but also that strong business and industry networks exist in the area. Include a dedicated page for leading employers and provide additional information on at least five employers (e.g., description of company operations and current employment). For bonus points, include links to company success stories.

    Notice I didn't just say "Major Employers." Our content historically refers to the companies with the most employees in our community, but that could be limiting information, especially in rural areas. Utilize a mix of diverse industry information in your content to show that your community is not a one-trick pony. Perhaps you have very innovative agri-businesses, some advanced manufacturing, and several new young technology services companies. Why would you promote only the ones that employ the most people over the companies that pay high wages but may have fewer employees? There is a way to do both. In fact, you can automatically rotate featured companies on your site, allowing even more stories to be shared than on one landing page.

4. **Provide Clear & Direct Contact Information**
    If a contact form or general email is the only way to contact your organization, your community will miss out on big opportunities. Site selectors and corporate executives are most likely to contact EDOs for the first time after developing a shortlist to request specific information or arrange a visit. When they're ready to

make that call, a decision-maker wants to be able to get on the phone with the right contact—ideally with the phone number easily found within one click (or less) from the homepage. Make sure to provide comprehensive contact details (direct phone, email, title) for key members, along with a photo so site visitors know exactly who they're talking to.

They do *not* fill out forms.

As an economic development consultant, when I'm trying to reach a community because I have a prospect interested in their region, and I can't find the contact information of the right person, I'm already frustrated before we have even begun. Have your contact information clearly displayed on the website and in your email signature. There is simply way too much competition out there to miss out over something as simple as this.

I've heard the excuses:
1. We have different people checking that email box.
2. We don't want spammers to have our direct email addresses or phone numbers.
3. If they are really interested in us, they will find us somehow…

Let me say candidly: to the outside world, these excuses look arrogant and lazy. Be bold. Put your name out there. Get some software to weed out the spammers. I can speak for all of my site selector clients (and myself) when I say that I'm not reaching out to any email address addressed to "info" or "admin." Who do I even ask for when I call? And I'm not filling out a form. Also, make sure that if I'm calling the city, I'm not getting directed to the water department or the police department. (Yes, this is more common than you know.)

Companies, prospects, and visitors can't wait to get to know you.

But they have to find you first.

Make it easy for them.

5. **Put Incentives Front and Center**

   Be sure to provide a comprehensive overview of state and local incentives—again, ideally within 1–2 clicks from the homepage. You don't have to go into great detail, but having the information on the site shows two things:

   1. Your community is serious about being a partner in a company's economic success.
   2. Your economic development representatives are knowledgeable about the programs and resources available to potential projects.

Note: Add a disclaimer or footnote at the bottom of this section to say something like "All projects must meet a minimum threshold / certain criteria to be considered for local, state, or federal incentives."

6. **Available Sites**

   Information on available sites is something every comprehensive EDO site should have—whether it's a dedicated page or a link to a separate provider. Using graphics and maps is a plus. This is the hardest thing to maintain, but it is critical to the outside world. You can't sell the community if you have nothing to show.

   If you only have raw land available (not shovel-ready), then I advise using renditions, digital graphics, drone aerial photos, and motion graphics to show what could take place on that site. Showing nothing makes you look either "full" or "invisible." We know you are neither, so this is important to consider. Likewise, if you have an industrial park, business park, or business district, be sure to promote them as well. I know my prospects also like to see the properties that were sold or leased and are thriving. A photo of a building that looks great and is productive with a "sold" or "leased" stamp over the top is a good visual for the community.

7. **Latest News**

   Keep visitors up to date on what's going on in your region by posting the latest announcements, events, and accolades. Try to post at least two updates per month (if not more), and make sure external news (i.e., company relocations and expansions) outweighs internal news (events, local updates, etc.). Also, include pertinent regional news. As mentioned before, prospects don't consider hard and fast boundaries the way locals do. This will raise your profile and show that you're a strong partner at the regional level.

8. **Make It User-Friendly**

   You may have noticed the "one to two clicks" rule is becoming a pattern. As an exercise, have a colleague or peer who is unfamiliar with the site test whether they can find everything a site selector might need within two clicks of the homepage. If not, your site could be causing visitors unnecessary frustration, and a navigation makeover may be something to consider.

   Another absolute must for a successful EDO website: responsiveness across mobile devices. Now, do the two-click test on a smartphone. If users can't find key information just as easily on their mobile phone, your site may be underperforming.

9. **Keep Design Modern and Fresh**

   While this best practice may be considered somewhat subjective, there are a few good rules of thumb for making sure your site is looking its best. For one, using large, crisp images is a great way to dress up any site. Increasingly, "retina-quality" images — three hundred or more pixels per inch — are becoming the web industry standard. High-quality images, balanced with an appropriate amount of white space, bold colors, and text, create a great recipe for modern, fresh web design. Website development comes in a wide price range. I promise you can find one within your budget.

10. Words That Help Us Find You

It's widely accepted that if you're not in the top two or three AI or Google search results (in this case, when a user enters your community followed by "economic development"), you're losing out on site viewers. That's why SEO is arguably one of the most important aspects of web design. Take this into consideration when developing your content. Get the right words built into your message, and use them throughout the site in order to move up the SEO search list. Be specific, and freshen up your content often. This is definitely something that is in your control. Take advantage of it.

11. Promote Your Own Economic Development Identity

I see that many rural communities simply have a page on their local city's municipal website. This makes some sense if the economic development effort is located within the confines of city hall. However, I am still a big proponent of the economic development organization having its own website. You will never be able to capture the attention of your audience in an imaginative and effective way if your information is buried between pages on how to pay the water bill and the next month's city council agenda. You can use the EDO page on the city site to introduce your local economic developer, their photo, and their contact information (or the board of directors or committee members), but then provide a hotlink directly to a comprehensive economic development site.

Your branded EDO site will promote the assets of the city, the county, and the surrounding region. It will promote available sites for industrial and business growth. It will explain economic development programs, incentives, and resources. It will provide helpful information for entrepreneurs and potential small businesses. It will introduce the EDO board and staff. It will graphically show locator maps, drone videos, and business testimonies. It will provide links to all of the pertinent resources and partners in the community (city, county, schools, taxing entities, chamber of commerce, realtors, lenders, etc.). You are simply not able to do these things if you just have a landing page on the city's site. To be competitive with neighboring communities (and the 17,000 other rural cities in the U.S.), you have to be projecting your Sunday best.

The EDO is important to the community.

Embrace your identity.

Go big and be bold.

"But we don't have the staff or money to maintain an EDO-specific site," I hear you say.

I will respond by saying that you really can't afford *not* to figure this out. I get it. It's a predictable response. But if you aren't out there, front and center, promoting your community and its assets, you are invisible. Both internally and externally.

So hear me out. I built and have maintained two websites myself for the past seven years—one for my company, ACCELERATION by design LLC, and one for my Stand Up Rural America events. Even running a few extra bells and whistles on both of them, together the cost is only about $800 a year. I own multiple domains (for offense and defense), which run approximately $200 a year. I have three branded email addresses that cost approximately $500 a year. You can spend as much or as little as you want on building the initial website.

I've had several communities go to their local high schools and colleges to ask if their students could build a site as part of a project for class credit. I know communities that had local web service businesses trade the building of the site in return for discreet advertising on the site. Basic but effective sites can be built economically. A more complicated site with lots of moving parts would, of course, cost more. There is no lack of talented agencies that can help you with your economic development site.

My point is—cost should not be the reason your community does not have its own economic development website.

Listen, kids are smart. They know technology. And they have big imaginations. Your local businesses, especially those with services that would be of interest to your audience (realtors, lenders, storage, trucking, staffing, etc.), would also welcome the opportunity to partner with you on building your site.

Where there's a will, there's a way.

Side note: There are two things that will immediately make your community look unnecessarily "small":

1. Featuring your water tower as your main photo. Even with great graphics displayed on the tower, it will make a viewer wonder, "Is this the best you've got to show me?"; and
2. not having your own website.

Both are limiting scenarios.

On the previous topic of making everyone an ambassador, I had a client that partnered with the local ISD and asked their high school students to present suggestions for a local social media campaign promoting their community. They offered prize money and expected (or were hoping) to be wowed by one campaign. They were wowed by eight of the campaigns. So much so that they increased their prize money and adopted all eight campaigns, to be used in various social media and direct mail forums in different ways over the next few years.

To top it off, they learned more about the various students and their skills, hired them for summer internships and after-school work, and promoted their skills to other local businesses. To say that this initiative was a win–win for all involved is an understatement. Bonus: The students are learning what it takes to keep their community alive, growing, and exciting. They are more engaged and will be more civic-minded as they move forward in their lives.

Who is telling your story? What are they telling? Where is your story being told?

The most vibrant rural communities have figured out how to use every avenue and every ambassador to tell their amazing stories.

It's a big, big world out there. Start with Chapter One.

HELLO *world*

ECONOMIC DEVELOPMENT MARKETING AND BRANDING are vital parts of economic development, especially for rural communities. It's the shorthand that communicates who you are to people both inside and outside your community. When it works, it resonates emotionally with stakeholders, prospects, potential businesses, and residents by inviting them to see why you are different and why people should invest, work, and buy in your community.

Here are six principles to drive your strategic and creative work with branding and marketing for economic development.

Principle #1: Understand Your Stakeholders. Start by acknowledging that the audiences in economic development branding are often more complex than those in singular product branding. You are simultaneously representing your community and trying to reach targets far beyond your area. That means you have one local focus and another independent focus. Balancing the two takes intentional effort and specific goals.

Principle #2: Clarify Your Objective. Identify your target markets and specific audiences. Once you understand your targets, focus on what you want your outcomes to be. Economic initiatives can vary dramatically, from attracting more diverse businesses to creating jobs, stabilizing a downtown, or driving tourism. The strategy behind your branding and marketing efforts should align precisely with your vision and goals. Different topics require different types and avenues of outreach, and different audiences prefer to receive marketing in different ways. Know your audience and your vision, and incorporate that into your marketing decisions. One size does not fit all.

Principle #3: Differentiate Yourself. Avoid repetition or duplication of others. Economic development efforts often use the same words and appeal to the same feelings, regardless of geographic area. Just look at how everyone talks about the quality of life—that's not a differentiating point. Instead, drill down deeper and define what makes the business climate and quality of life unique and special in your area.

Principle #4: Avoid conflicting or redundant messaging. Have a common vision for the entire community. It is okay for different local groups to focus on different topics. However, if one organization is promoting the community's heritage, historical downtown, and historical neighborhoods, while another is highlighting modern housing and high-tech construction, the messaging becomes contradictory. The community may be an awesome mixture of both—so let that be your message instead of projecting completely conflicting narratives. Similarly, if the city is promoting a "low-taxes" message while the school district is advocating for a multi-million-dollar bond election, both can be true, but the messaging should be balanced to avoid direct contradiction.

Principle #5: Empower Your Community. While your brand should be believable and authentic, that does not mean boring. The community should understand that, when it comes to economic development, you cannot market what feels ordinary and safe. Aim to stand out. Be bold and be different.

Principle #6: Live the brand. Economic development is not just about nice pictures and words. It goes far beyond an engaging slogan. Instead, aim to live the brand through actions. If your brand is about small-town living with a nostalgic feel, your storefronts should reflect that, and your hospitality and retail workers should be welcoming. If your economic development brand is about diversity, your recruitment efforts for businesses should actively welcome people of all ethnicities and genders. If your efforts are focused on tourism, invest in attractions that make people want to return to your area over and over. Talk the talk and walk the walk.

Lesson Learned: Sadly, when budgets are tight, when the economy is down, or when apathy exists in a community, the first thing that gets cut is the marketing budget. But that's when it is more critical than ever to tell your story. Pitch your assets. Brag about your business climate. Promote your existing businesses. Creating consistent, engaging, and memorable marketing is what will get you to the front of the line. Without memorable marketing, you aren't even in the game because no one will know about your city.

Remember, people don't know what they don't know. You have to tell them. Don't be invisible — or worse, don't let a competitor define your identity or your viability.

The overarching objective of a marketing plan is to generate quality prospects, positive attention and remind the local citizens of the assets located in your city and your region.

- If the purpose of your economic development marketing is to lead to new investment and job creation, then your marketing priorities should concentrate on target industries that, based on your research, have the most advantages for locating in your community or your region.
- If you are marketing for new residents, then your marketing should reflect livability issues (housing, education, medical and connectivity) along with quality-of-life assets (events, recreation, arts, culture, clubs, etc.).
- If you are marketing for tourism, you should focus on retail, hospitality, recreation, food service, etc.

You get the drill. One marketing piece, one initiative, one message will not be sufficient. One size does not fit all. You might be pursuing all of those things. If so, you need three different messages and three different hot target audience lists. Just make sure that all of the marketing collateral is cohesive, branded, and coordinated.

Points to Ponder:

- Is your local EDC included in critical conversations about the future of the city?
- Does the EDC get invited to give presentations to local civic groups or regional groups?
- Does your city immediately come to mind when site selectors, brokers, or state and regional economic development agencies are presented with a prospect?

If the answer to these questions is no, then it is time to aggressively boost the profile of the economic development efforts among lead generators, decision-makers, stakeholders, residents, existing industry, realtors, elected officials, supporting agencies, and site selectors.

- Develop a series of communications about your city or county (available sites, workforce availability, education, cost of living, amenities, proximity etc.) and distribute it to the important stake-holders on a regular and consistent basis. This can be done in the form of editorials, newsletter, checking-in emails, blog posts, etc.
- Join and participate in pertinent organizations that involve strong stakeholders in the community, region, and state.
- Post photos on social media when attending important events, conferences, and meetings. It is important that the EDC is shown as busy, engaged, and working on behalf of the community.
- Develop a short VIP List of people who need to know when something impactful happens, such as the availability of a new site, a new workforce initiative, a company expansion, nearby announcements, new housing developments, school bonds for new facilities, favorable utility or road expansions, etc. This list would include elected officials, lead generation groups, site selectors, regional promoters, utility representatives, and state agency representatives.

Consistent Communication. Consistent Messaging. Interesting Content.

And a big mouth.

That's all you need.

Let's go.

FINE-TUNE
the message

CITIES, COUNTIES, REGIONS, AND STATES can thrive only when they embrace a sustainable, long-term development trajectory by inviting the best minds and businesses to work together. This is achieved by effectively communicating the opportunities for growth available to new residents, skilled workers, and businesses. The narrative built to attract these drivers of growth ultimately shapes the future of these places.

The opportunity to create an exciting and dynamic digital presence is within reach. Remember, if I can't find information before my first visit to your community, how would a prospect, a potential resident, a remote worker, or a tourist find you? Being a "best-kept secret" is the worst economic development marketing tactic in the world.

Messaging Advice:
- Your message should accompany *actual* development—economic, community, and social development. You can't just say you are doing it; you have to actually do it.
- Your branding and messaging provide an opportunity for cities to reimagine and reposition themselves, possibly overcoming invisibility, an unfavorable image, or a difficult past. It is a chance to create your own dynamic image and drive growth on your own, favorable terms. You control your story, and you control your message.

- Be real. Being honest and realistic about the opportunities available or offered in your community or your region helps to attract the right talent and to drive economic development.
- Your story is built on what your region, county, or city aspires to be. This, in turn, prompts stakeholders to work towards becoming what is being projected and ensures development efforts are aligned with the overall direction (the big picture or vision).
- Your community's branding and messaging can build a sense of belonging and cohesiveness among new residents and locals alike.
- Your branding should include tenants like talent attraction, tourism, and economic development. Those often still operate in silos. Your efforts can connect the dots and bring different players together around a shared vision and theme.

Branding, marketing, and messaging are so much more than just a brochure, a picture, or a post. It's the meshing of multiple forums and avenues of outreach, designated for both internal and external audiences, and scheduled to provide consistent bites of data, visuals, and information.

Lesson Learned: It's just as important to develop internal marketing regarding your assets and opportunities as it is external outreach for a number of reasons:

- Your available sites may attract a local entrepreneur or investor.
- A business employee or hospitality representative may have the first contact with a prospective business, resident, or tourist.
- Good things are contagious. If your community is informed and included in the messaging, then they become your best ambassadors.

Every person has a story. Every business has a story. Every city has a story.

I know you have a great story to tell. An interesting story to tell. A poignant story to tell. An exciting story to tell. Buried deep inside every community is a great story to tell.

And I can't wait to hear it.

EXPECT
the unexpected

I WISH I COULD TELL YOU that every project I've worked on or every community I've worked with has been fun and games—sunshine and unicorns—and rewarding beyond words. But it hasn't been. Pursuing economic development is not for the faint of heart. And there is a lot of heartburn that goes along with the occasional win, incremental progress, or tangible success.

Getting a community to a point of sustainability is difficult. Getting it to a point of growth and activity is even harder. Getting it to a point of consistent vibrancy and excellence is working at a whole other level. It's not impossible, but it requires tremendous vision, commitment, and fortitude.

Pursuing economic development can feel like a pipe dream in rural communities, where the number of active community members is often limited, leadership is spread thin, and resources are in demand. The community may be doing everything it can just to keep the train on the tracks. It is not in a position to talk about building a new track or a shiny new train.

And then, just when you think you have it all together, the unexpected happens. A plant closes. The school bond fails. A main water line breaks. An empty downtown building caves in. The community throws a bunch of time and money into pursuing a project that ends up in a neighboring city. Morale is low. Houses are empty. Consumers look elsewhere for products. It's easy to see that, sadly, this is when the population slide begins.

We have to expect the unexpected. Create contingency plans. Be proactive instead of reactive. If you have a strong business retention and expansion program, you might have a heads-up about the plant closing. You might have time to help the company reverse course and save the jobs. If the closing is out of your control, can you quickly put together a job fair for employees who are now out of work? Can you implement training programs to help re-skill this newly available workforce? Are you aware of other companies in the region that could absorb some of the displaced employees so they can continue to commute and remain in the community? Does the city have a designated fund for infrastructure emergencies? Does the city have safety ordinances in place to prevent buildings from becoming so dilapidated that their roofs cave in? Does the EDC have strong regional relationships so that, if your city loses a project to a neighboring city, you can still attract new residents and taxpayers or help existing citizens commute to new opportunities?

While we constantly look to improve our communities, we must always remember that the unexpected can happen at any time—an ammonia spill, a pandemic, plant closings, or natural disasters.

Just as we, as individuals, prepare for emergencies by having wills, powers of attorney, DNRs, trusts, and estate plans, we should do the same for our communities. Stay the course and work your plan. Be realistic and be prepared for the unexpected.

I'm not advocating that you work yourself into a constant state of worry. I am the epitome of optimism and the opposite of gloom and doom. But I am a realist. The quicker you can get back on track, assist the community, or hold down the fort, the better. If it takes only hours or days to react to a community emergency instead of months, you will make it. You will survive it. You will learn from it. And you will bounce back from it.

How we react to unexpected challenges could be the difference between growth, sustainability, or population slide.

When working with EDC boards or city councils, I use a list of twenty plausible crisis scenarios to start the conversation. It's an eye-opening and helpful exercise. Many find that they are much better prepared than they thought they were—and many are glad to have the hard conversations in times of calm instead of in times of crisis.

Crisis is going to happen. It might be on a small scale, or it can happen on a large scale. But no community is immune from crisis. Natural disasters, fires, wrecks, an economic downturn, a bust in commodity prices, loss of jobs, etc. They are a part of life. But how we deal with them can be the deciding factor in how your community bounces back, moves on or gets stuck in a purgatory of inaction.

The most vibrant communities are the ones that recognize that everything is not always easy. Things don't always go as planned. I've always advised my clients and members to use 70% of their budget on their plan, their targets, their initiatives, their marketing, and their programs. Then, allocate 20% of their budget for the unexpected opportunities, unsolicited prospects, and when they need to be reactive to good things that materialize outside of their program of work. That leaves 10% for the safety zone. The unexpected. A crisis. Because having the ability to react quickly is critical to what happens next.

But having the hard discussion about who is going to take the lead if unexpected things happen is just as important as having the resources to deal with it quickly.

Being prepared for the unexpected will put you in a position to enjoy the freedom to be ambitious and aggressive in your economic development and growth initiatives.

Have the hard discussion now so you can aggressively move forward with a clear heart, a clear mission, and a plan filled with contingency and purpose.

Peace of mind is a priceless resource.

LET'S GO...

GO FORTH *and conquer*

THANK YOU FOR READING THIS FAR. This book was designed to give you something to think about. To help you process the opportunities and challenges that our rural communities are living right now. To give you new perspectives on where we've been, what we're doing, and what lies ahead.

If you are in a rural community that feels stuck, is having a hard time getting off high center, or is suffering from apathy, I hope that you found a few nuggets in this book that will inspire you to fight for your community, to take action, to make a difference, because you hold the power.

If you are in a rural community that is fighting to survive, much less thrive, let me share with you a mantra I believe in and have used in my work every single day for the past 34 years.

Dream Big—Start Small

Dream big. Go crazy. Use your wildest imagination when thinking about what your rural community can become. Because when you dream big and find your fellow crazy believers, the magic begins to happen. Okay, it's easy to say, "Dream big." But economic development, community development, and social development are all daunting projects—extremely daunting. Where do you even start? How do we bounce back? How do we move the train forward?

My advice is to start small. Baby steps. Small bites. Little projects. Do something that creates a vision, sparks action, and builds enthusiasm. Stop meeting and whining about it—just do something because small somethings turn into bigger somethings. Small somethings create pride and belief in your direction. Before long, more people will want to be part of the *something* that is going to improve the community. Too many communities do the opposite: they dream small but start too big. Their unrealistic expectations for success immediately put achievement out of reach.

Picture your community building a beautiful brick fence. Lay the foundation (the vision), then start building it one brick at a time.

Dream big. Start small. Tangible wins, increased enthusiasm, pride, and more action will follow.

Honor Your History, but Build for Your Future

I know you have heard me mention this multiple times throughout the book, but I firmly believe it with all my heart: Our rural communities are built on the incredible history of our country—the innovators, the pioneers, the risk-takers, the builders, the dreamers, the visionaries. We must never forget what the generations before us endured to create this dynamic country. They built our beautiful town squares, our brick streets, our majestic grain elevators, our neighborhoods, our schools, and our factories. They dug the trenches for our water lines, raised the poles for our electricity, and mined for our precious minerals. They fought tirelessly for our towns, our families, our neighbors, and our businesses. We must never forget that. We honor their fortitude and their commitment to what makes Rural America so great.

But time does not stand still for us. Our needs and opportunities continue to evolve, and we must adapt with them. That doesn't mean sacrificing our history in the name of progress. Instead, it is because of history that we are able to grow and thrive in a new century, with new assets and new dreams.

Many cities have managed to roll with the punches and make the necessary changes to thrive. They are comfortable with who they are, where they came from, and what lies ahead. To those rural communities, we say cheers and congratulate them on their diligence and inspiration. We celebrate them, learn from them, and lift them up as examples of our great nation.

For those cities that have struggled to turn the page, stop the slide, or find a new dream—it is never too late. It's never too late *if* you want things to change for the better. But you have to *want* it. I can help you all day long with the nuts and bolts of how to get unstuck, how to take small, actionable steps, and how to work together toward a fresh approach. But I can't make you want it.

I see beauty, assets, and opportunities everywhere I go. I see them in every small town I drive through or work in—even in those places others have given up on.

It's never too late to turn the page.

You can honor your history, but build for the future. It's not an either/or proposition. You can do both.

Never Stop Believing

I have seen cities recover from natural disasters, schools rebuilt after being demolished by fire, cities decimated by plant closings resurge with new industries, and cities recover from corruption, collusion, and scandal. Any of these scenarios could have been the death of a city—and sadly, sometimes they are. But I am a believer in people and in the power of controlling one's own destiny.

Recently, a friend visited a very popular city in Central Texas and commented to me about how *lucky* they were that their city was so vibrant. I said, "Did you say *lucky?*"

And she said, "Yes, I said lucky..."

In a very nice way (because my head wanted to explode), I explained to her that economic development is not about luck. Okay, *sometimes* they get lucky—but only because they have put themselves in a position to attract that luck.

I had to tell her that I remember that community from 40 years ago. It was near where I went to college, and it was nothing like the bustling, vibrant place it is today. Four decades ago, the city council, along with a group of citizens, gathered and decided they wanted *more* for their city. They wanted to work toward a vision. They were too far from any metro area to be a bedroom community. They were not on major highways that would naturally attract manufacturing or industrial projects. But they were a community filled with pride—for their heritage, their homes, and the Hill Country.

They debated and discussed until they developed a twenty-year plan that included all the infrastructure needed to transform their city from a simple stopover into a true destination for Hill Country visitors. They envisioned a downtown filled with shops, restaurants, and historical markers. They wanted it to be pedestrian-friendly and open on evenings and weekends. They wanted people to come and stay awhile.

Forty years ago, this seemed like a pipe dream. Since then, multiple city council members and business owners have come and gone. There have been property disputes, arguments over *how* to get things done, fights about parking, curfews, dogs, and alcohol. Believe me, their road to greatness was not a walk in the park. But they never lost sight of the end goal. They never deviated from the adopted mission, and it has paid off in spades.

It wasn't easy, but it was worth it. It wasn't *luck* that got them there. It was vision, hard work, blood, sweat, tears, and dollars. And, of course, after the twenty-year plan was complete, they continued to grow, making adjustments and evolving with the times, the market, and the economy.

So forgive me if I get a little protective of a city when someone casually says, "They are so lucky." I know how hard they worked to get where they are. I have watched it happen for forty years. And I know that other cities can do the same.

We'll take all the luck we can get. But you still have to believe.

You just have to believe that your city is worth fighting for.

Quit Waiting for a Hero to Come in and Save You

In closing, I beseech you: please take the words "if only" out of your thought process. In the hundreds of cities I have worked with over the decades, this is the one phrase that is the hardest nut to crack. It's even worse than "We've tried it before, and it failed" or "That's how we've always done it." Those phrases can be easily debunked, reframed, and turned into a catalyst for better things to come. But if you are stuck in an "if only" state of mind, it's much harder to get you to see a vision of how great, how vibrant, and how dynamic your city can be.

An "if only" mindset puts you in the "poor me" or "no one loves us" zone. Early on, I realized that during board retreats or town hall meetings, once one person started their comments with "If only..." the discussion almost always went downhill. And then it was like *Lord of the*

Flies—the whole conversation spiraled into blame and negativity. *If only a business had stayed, if only someone took care of their building, if only they had ten new houses, if only the interstate didn't bypass them, if only the bank would lend more money, if only they had a better football team, if only the coffee shop had doughnuts—if only, if only, if only...*

So, I started bringing an hourglass with me that took five minutes to empty. I would tell them, "Let's get the *if onlys* out of the way." Then, we'd fill up a chart with as many *if onlys* as they could think of in five minutes. At the end of those five minutes, we'd quickly review the list and categorize each item—what's plausible, what's real, what's junk, and what's just drivel. And then, we'd move on. No more *if onlys* allowed after that.

It's amazing how quickly attitudes shift when people hear themselves say their "if only" out loud. In five minutes, we could usually go around the room twice. The first time, responses were often whiny and unrealistic. But by the second time, answers became more measured, thoughtful, and plausible. There's a big difference between "If only someone would create 30 jobs" and "If only we had more lights on Main Street."

You see where I'm going with this? Blaming the state of your community on something abstract will get you nowhere. But reframing your thoughts into something actionable and realistic? That's a whole new ball game.

If you were deciding where to invest your money, would you invest in your own community? If yes, then let's figure out the best use of your investment—the best ROI, the best way to leverage it with other funds for a great project.

If you would not invest in your own community, let me ask you this: why would you expect someone else to? Quit waiting for someone to come in and save you. You, as a community, have the ability and the responsibility to invest in yourselves. It is not someone else's obligation to come in and invest in something that you aren't willing to invest in yourself.

You've got to have skin in the game. You've got to have commitment. Because when you start investing in your community, that's when others will line up to join you.

Be the hero of your own story.

Stand Up Rural America.

This is your time. The opportunities are real. The spotlight is on you.

I'm excited for what lies ahead for you.

The question is: Are you ready?

If you are ready for growth and prosperity, then *take action!* If you are struggling to take baby steps, *you got this!* If you are stuck and don't know where to start, *start small.* If you are rockin' it and running on full cylinders, *keep going!*

I believe in Rural America. And I believe in you.

Let's go!

ABOUT LORIE

LORIE VINCENT IS a certified economic developer with over three decades of experience in the field. Throughout her career, she has developed organizational strategies, dynamic prospect events, and memorable marketing initiatives that have aided in the creation of thousands of jobs and billions of dollars in capital investment.

Having worked with more than 20 different industries, domestic and abroad, her knowledge of economic trends and opportunities is extensive. Comfortable in both cowboy boots and a hard hat or a suit and stilettos, she has worked with the smallest of cities to the largest of states. While Lorie is a certified economic developer, she considers her more than quarter century of "in the trenches" experience her most potent, tangible, and resourceful asset.

Professional Trailblazer

Lorie has taken three EDOs to the "next level": one at the local level (Sherman County), one at a sixty-nine-county regional level (The High Ground of Texas), and one at the state level (Team Texas). Her creativity, ingenuity, and understanding of different value propositions have resulted in diverse and unique marketing strategies, world-renowned VIP hospitality events, and impactful keynote presentations.

She is the architect of the popular ACCELERATOR Training Programs, the Trade Show Acceleration Series, the Bringing New Life to Old Bricks-Downtown Revitalization Workshop, and the popular Stand Up Rural America Summit. Lorie has coordinated over 300 trade shows, excursions & industry events all over the globe. She does not ask "why" but rather "why not?" And don't tell her it can't be done… That's like a double dog dare you challenge!

Professional Consensus Builder

Lorie has worked with more than four hundred and fifty cities, counties, chambers, associations, utilities, cooperatives, and state agencies. More than a facilitator or goal setter, she believes in vigorous action plans with measurable results. She has raised over six million dollars for her organizations by developing aggressive, innovative, and cutting-edge forward planning, membership, and marketing objectives.

Lorie's bold approach, paired with her strong belief in collaboration, has allowed her to build the support of thousands of stakeholders for specific outreach programs and dynamic marketing initiatives. She has a gift of making each prospect, member, and audience feel special. And she loves dogs, tacos, George Strait, and macaroni and cheese.

Professional Storyteller

Boy, does Lorie have some stories! A popular speaker, writer & trainer, her real-life escapades, successes, challenges, and "well, that was embarrassing" moments are absorbed into a strong message of fun and inspiration. She's a strong advocate for rural America, a true believer in regionalism, a cheerleader for existing business appreciation, a big strategic thinker, a kick-butt party planner, a professional rule-breaker, and a chaos coordinator. Her knowledge runs deep, and her enthusiasm is contagious! In addition to speaking to more than five hundred groups throughout her career, her long-awaited books, *Stand Up Rural America: Forging a New Path of Growth & Prosperity and Mayhem & Mishaps: Tales of a Small Town Girl in a Big 'Ole World,* are scheduled for release in Summer of 2025.

THANK YOU FOR READING MY BOOK!

I hope this book will serve as a catalyst to start the discussion and, more importantly, the ACTION towards a more vibrant and sustainable community.

If you would like to continue the journey to prosperity together, please reach out, and let's make it happen!

HERE ARE A FEW WAYS WE CAN **move forward together...**

Order copies of Stand Up Rural America for Your Team or Organization

Would you like to buy multiple copies of the book to share with your team, your boards, your elected officials, or your members? Contact us at LorieSpeaks@accelerationbydesign.com to learn about bulk discounts, bonuses, and special offers – customized to meet your needs.

Speaking and Workshop Bundles

If you were inspired by the concepts in the book, I'd love to bring them to your next event or conference. From standalone keynotes to workshops to book bundle packages, everything is customized to your audience and your needs. In addition to topics directly related to the Stand Up Rural America book, I also offer the Downtown Revitalization Workshop-Bringing New Life to Old Bricks, Trade Show Acceleration Series, The Business Boost Program, the Community Tune-Up Program, and more.

Learn about the Stand Up Rural America signature keynote (as well as other popular presentations and services) at www.accelerationbydesign.com/the-speaker.

ACCELERATION by design LLC is a boutique economic development firm that provides consulting, facilitation, training, member engagement, and organizational effectiveness services to cities, regions, and states across the U.S.

Want to read Stand Up Rural America as part of a book club?
Grab the companion guide at www.accelerationbydesign.com/suracompanion for prompts and questions you can discuss. Beer and tacos—optional.

Podcasts, Blogs and Interviews
I love to talk about the greatness of Rural America! I'm thrilled for the opportunity to talk about how amazing our Rural Communities are and how we can all work together to reach economic sustainability and prosperity! It's time to celebrate the stories of Rural Trailblazers!

Let's Connect!
Facebook:
www.facebook.com/lorie.barbervincent/
www.facebook.com/accelerationbydesign/
www.facebook.com/lorievincent.speaker/

LinkedIn:
www.linkedin.com/in/lorie-vincent1

Instagram:
www.instagram.com/loravincent1

You are invited to join the Stand Up Rural America Community
You can find our free Facebook community at:
www.Facebook.com/groups/StandUpRuralAmerica/
Inside this community, you will find thousands of Rural Trailblazers just like you who are making a difference every day in their homes, their businesses, their communities, their regions, and their states. You will find shared resources, case studies, programs, inspiration and, most importantly, understanding. What we do and what we are working for is noble, but hard. These are your people. Join us as we lift up and celebrate all that Rural America has to offer!

Just to say thanks for buying and reading my book, I would like to give you a few free bonus gifts, no strings attached!

Scan the QR Code:

I appreciate your interest in my book and value your feedback as it helps me improve future versions of this book. I would appreciate it if you could leave your invaluable review on Amazon.com with your feedback.
Thank you!